THE DOOR TO SATISFACTION

The Heart Advice of a Tibetan Buddhist Master

The Door to Satisfaction

The Heart Advice of a Tibetan Buddhist Master

BY

Lama Thubten Zopa Rinpoche

Given in the holy place of Bodhgaya, India, and based on
*Opening the Door of Dharma: The Initial Stage of Training the Mind in the
Graduated Path to Enlightenment,* a collection of advice of the great Kadampas,
compiled by Lodrö Gyaltsen, a fifteenth-century Tibetan yogi

Foreword by
KIRTI TSENSHAB RINPOCHE

Edited by
AILSA CAMERON & ROBINA COURTIN

WISDOM PUBLICATIONS ❧ BOSTON

WISDOM PUBLICATIONS
361 NEWBURY STREET
BOSTON, MASSACHUSETTS 02115

Library of Congress Cataloging-in-Publication Data

Thubten Zopa, Rinpoche, 1946–
    The door to satisfaction : the heart advice of a Tibetan Buddhist master / by
    Lama Thubten Zopa Rinpoche ; edited by Ailsa Cameron and Robina Courtin.
        p.   cm.
    "Given in the holy place of Bodhgaya, India, and based on Opening the door of
    dharma: The Initial stage of training the mind in the graduated path to enlighten-
    ment, a collection of advice of the great Kadampas, compiled by Lodrö Gyaltsen,
    a fifteenth-century Tibetan yogi."
    Includes bibliographical references.
    ISBN 0-86171-058-4 (pbk. : acid-free paper) :
    1. Spiritual life—Bka'-gdams-pa (Sect) 2. Lam-rim. 3. Blo-gros-rgyal-mtshan,
    Spyaṅ-sṅa, 1402–1471. Opening the door of dharma.
    I. Cameron, Ailsa. II. Courtin, Robina. III. Blo-gros-rgyal-mtshan, Spyaṅ-sṅa,
    1402–1471. Opening the door of dharma. IV. Title.
    BQ7670.6.T49 1994
    294.3'444--dc20   93-35945

    99 98 97 96 95
    6   5   4   3   2

Cover photography: © 1993 by Clive Arrowsmith, London, England
The publisher offers heartfelt thanks to Clive Arrowsmith
for once again sharing his beautiful photographs.

⟶⟨ॐ⟩⟵

Set at Wisdom Publications in Adobe Garamond & Adobe Garamond Expert
Collection, Bullfinch and Diacritical Garamond by Orpheus Korshak.

Designed by: L·J·SAWLit'

Printed in the United States of America.

Contents

Sponsors' Dedication

MAY THE MERIT of sponsoring this publication ensure the long lives of Lama Thubten Zopa Rinpoche, Lama Tenzin Ösel Rinpoche, and all the Sangha of the Foundation for the Preservation of the Mahayana Tradition (FPMT), and benefit all those sentient beings who have passed away serving others.

The publisher thanks Henry and Catherine for arranging the sponsorship of this book, and our kind well-wishers in Singapore and Dr. Don Brown for contributing to its publication.

Foreword

About a thousand years ago in Tibet, the incomparable Atisha, author of the text *Lamp on the Path to Enlightenment,* founded the precious Kadampa tradition. His closest disciple was Dromtön Gyalwai Jungne, whose coming was foretold by the goddess Tara. Dromtönpa's three foremost followers, one of whom was Potowa Rinchen Sel, were renowned as the three Kadam brothers. Geshe Langri Tangpa Dorje Seng-ge was a direct disciple of Geshe Potowa.

It was through these masters that the essence of this experiential tradition—the subduing of the eight worldly dharmas, the spurning of the concerns of this present existence and the training in the mind of enlightenment by way of cherishing others above self—came to be revered as the most precious practice of the early Kadam tradition.

The New Kadam tradition was handed down by the great Lama Tsong Khapa and his main spiritual son, Khedrub Rinpoche. One of their direct followers was Chen-nga Lodrö Gyaltsen, and it was he who composed the present text, *Opening the Door of Dharma: The Initial Stage of Training the Mind in the Graduated Path to Enlightenment.*

This work is akin to a key that opens the entrance to that class of instructions that encourages beginning practitioners to turn their thoughts towards Dharma. As such it will prove highly beneficial to those who are interested. In the case of Lama Zopa Rinpoche it has acted as the basis of some very genuine Dharma experience.

I therefore wholeheartedly welcome and rejoice at the appearance of these teachings on the text. I would also like to offer a sincere prayer that this book will contribute to the turning of the thoughts of all beings towards the Dharma and lead them swiftly to the joy and peace of enlightenment.

Kirti Tsenshab Rinpoche
Dharamsala, India

Editors' Preface

*I*N FEBRUARY 1990 MORE THAN a hundred students of Buddhism from all over the world gathered in a large multicolored tent on the grounds of Root Institute, a Buddhist center in the ancient Indian town of Bodhgaya, where two and a half thousand years ago the Buddha himself achieved enlightenment.

The event was a series of teachings given as part of the Third Enlightened Experience Celebration, a periodic festival of Buddhist teachings and initiations organized by the Foundation for the Preservation of the Mahayana Tradition.

From February 16 to 25, Lama Thubten Zopa Rinpoche, the Spiritual Director of the FPMT, gave "The Kadampa Teachings," a series of ten discourses based on the fifteenth-century text of the Tibetan yogi Lodrö Gyaltsen, *Opening the Door of Dharma.*

Lama Zopa startled his audience by declaring that it was only after reading this text in his late twenties that he understood the real meaning of practicing Dharma. This was startling because everyone present knew from their years of experience as Rinpoche's students, or from his reputation, that in fact every moment of his life had been devoted to Dharma, to spiritual practice; that he was a perfect example of a Dharma practitioner. Clearly, there was something meaningful to be listened to here.

As Rinpoche himself recounts in the Prologue to this book, he was born in 1946 in the Solu Khumbu region of Nepal, near Mount Everest. According to his mother, from the time he could speak, he would often declare, "I am the Lawudo Lama." This lama, Kunsang Yeshe, who had died in 1945, was famous in the area as a highly realized ascetic practitioner. For the last twenty years of his life he had lived and meditated in a nearby cave at Lawudo and had been the spiritual mentor of the local people. It was said that his energy to serve others was inexhaustible, and that, like all great yogis, he had passed beyond the need for sleep.

Indeed, the young boy was recognized as the reincarnation. The Lawudo Lama's main disciple, Ngawang Chöpel, had, in the traditional manner, consulted various high lamas in Tibet, who had all agreed on the finding. In addition, Rinpoche correctly identified articles belonging to the Lawudo Lama.

In the Prologue Rinpoche tells us about his early life, first in Nepal, at Thami monastery, and later in Rolwaling, and eventually in Tibet, at the monastery of Domo Geshe Rinpoche in Pagri. The Lawudo Lama had been a Nyingma yogi, a layman, but it was at Domo Geshe's monastery that Lama Zopa Rinpoche first met the Gelug teachings of Tibetan Buddhism and where he became a monk. The Dharma Protector associated with the monastery also confirmed that Rinpoche was a reincarnate lama and offered advice concerning his care.

After three years in Pagri, Lama Zopa decided to go to Sera Monastery, one of the great Gelug monastic universities near Lhasa, to continue his studies. However, the Dharma Protector fortuitously advised Rinpoche not to go, but instead to do a meditation retreat. It was at this time, in 1959, when Rinpoche was thirteen, that the Chinese communists suppressed the Tibetan uprising in Lhasa against their continued presence in Tibet and took over the government of the country.

As Rinpoche explains, when the arrival of the Chinese at Pagri was imminent, he escaped through Bhutan to India, to Buxa Duar in West Bengal. Here he remained for eight years, continuing his studies with hundreds of other refugee lamas, monks, and nuns in what had been a concentration camp at the time of the British.

It was here that Rinpoche came under the care of a Sera Monastery monk, Lama Thubten Yeshe, with whom he would remain as his heart disciple until 1984, when Lama Yeshe passed away. "Lama Yeshe was more than a father, more than a mother," Rinpoche says. "Like a mother hen feeding her chick from her own mouth, Lama took care of me."

During the following twenty years, these two lamas would have an immense impact on the Western world, attracting thousands of students through the power of their teachings and the tireless compassion of their extensive activities to benefit others.

They met their first Western student in Darjeeling in 1965, while Rinpoche was recuperating from tuberculosis. An American citizen, Zina Rachevsky was the daughter of a Romanov prince who had escaped to France during the Russian Revolution. She began receiving teachings from Lama Yeshe, with Rinpoche translating for her in his newly learned English. Both lamas would later teach exclusively in English to their Western students.

In 1968, with Zina now ordained as a nun, they moved together to Nepal. It was here that the lamas' powerful connection with Westerners was to develop in earnest. At first they lived in Baudhanath just outside Kathmandu, the site of an ancient Buddhist stupa. From their house, according to Rinpoche, "every day Lama would look out through the window at a particular hill" in the distance, to the north across the terraced fields of the valley. "He seemed very attracted to it, and one day we went out to check that hill. It was the Kopan hill."

Kopan had been the home of the astrologer to the King of Nepal, and the lamas moved there in 1969. The following year, Rinpoche accepted the request of his relatives to return to Solu Khumbu, and during his visit there, Lawudo Cave and all the belongings of the Lawudo Lama were returned to him by the previous lama's son. It was also during this visit that Rinpoche fulfilled a promise made by the Lawudo Lama to start a monastic school for the young boys of the region. Rinpoche called it Mount Everest Centre.

In 1971, Rinpoche gave his first public teachings, at Kopan, to a group of twelve Westerners—an intensive introduction to Buddhist philosophy and meditation. This was the first of what has become an annual event that attracts hundreds of participants from around the world.

Westerners, tired of their materialism and hungry for something to activate their inner aspirations, were deeply moved by the clear-sighted, practical, and compassionate methods of Mahayana Buddhism. These were not empty words but a living tradition of teachings and meditation practices that stretched back in an unbroken line of master and disciple to the Buddha himself. And the methods clearly worked: this was evident from being with the lamas, from hearing their teachings, listening to their personal advice, observing them with others. They were literally full of the human qualities of patience, kindness, humor, wisdom, and contentment.

The lamas accepted the invitations of their growing number of students and visited the West for the first time in 1974. The first stop on their teaching tour of the United States, Australia, and New Zealand was New York. "But it wasn't a big shock," relates Rinpoche, "because I was familiar with it through studying English from *Time* magazines and through meeting so many Westerners, young and old, and hearing their life experiences."

After the lamas' visits, students in various countries began to open up centers for Dharma teachings and meditation, and in 1975 Lama Yeshe named this fledgling network the Foundation for the Preservation of the Mahayana Tradition (FPMT). Kopan was the wellspring of this activity. Each year Rinpoche would give what had become known as the "November Course." And each year the lamas would travel from Kopan to an ever-growing number of places in response to more and more invitations to teach.

By now Mount Everest Centre had moved down from the mountains to Kopan in the Kathmandu valley, and this facility for the monastic education of Sherpas, Manangpas, Tsumpas, and others from Nepal, as well as Tibetans, continued to expand.

In 1973, while in meditation retreat in the mountains of Nepal, Zina Rachevsky died as a result of an illness. According to Rinpoche, there were many signs at her death to indicate that she had achieved spiritual realizations.

The following year, during a visit to Lawudo Cave, Rinpoche discovered the text that is the basis of this book, the one that convinced him that only after reading it did he find out "how to practice Dharma."

So, what is it about this text that moved this great spiritual practitioner to say that? As Rinpoche explains, *Opening the Door of Dharma* "is the first thing to practice if you want to practice Dharma."

The essential point, which Rinpoche states right at the beginning and clarifies throughout the book, is that whether or not something is a spiritual practice is not determined by the type of activity, such as meditating or praying or reciting scriptures; it is determined by the reason, the motivation, for doing it. He points out that a so-called spiritual activity is not a Dharma activity—in other words, does not bring a positive result—if it is motivated by desire, by attachment to some mundane result here and now. And conversely, even a so-called worldly activity is a Dharma activity if it is done with a more expansive, long-term motivation.

As far as Mahayana Buddhism is concerned, the most expansive motivation for doing anything is the wish to achieve enlightenment so that one can lead others to this state of peerless wisdom and compassion. This approach is unique to the Mahayana, the path of the *bodhisattvas*—those who possess effortless *bodhicitta*, the mind of enlightenment; in other words, a spontaneous and continuous Mahayana motivation. Various methods for achieving bodhicitta are precisely outlined in the graduated path to enlightenment (in Tibetan, *lam-rim*), a step-by-step presentation of Buddha's teachings first taught in Tibet by the great Lama Atisha in the eleventh century.

Another powerful approach to developing bodhicitta is the set of teachings and meditations known as thought transformation or mind training (in Tibetan, *lo-jong*). The special emphasis here is on the practice of exchanging oneself for others, in other words, cherishing others instead of cherishing oneself. In general, one learns to use every moment of life, whether happy or unhappy, to destroy self-cherishing, the greatest obstacle to bodhicitta.

Pabongka Dechen Nyingpo explains in *Liberation in the Palm of Your Hand*:

> [Thought transformation] is able to dispel the darkness of self-cherishing, just as even a fraction of the rays of the sun can dispel darkness. It can dispel the disease of self-cherishing just as even a part of the medicine tree can dispel illness. In these times when the five types of degeneration are commonplace and other Dharma may not be effective, this mind training will help you, and you will not be bothered by unfortunate circumstances. This Dharma has so many greatnesses. (pp. 588–589)

These teachings derive from the eighth-century Indian Mahayana master Shantideva, who exhorted yogis to practice them in secret, because, as Pabongka Dechen Nyingpo says, they would not be "to the liking of an unfit vessel."

It was Lama Atisha who also brought these teachings to Tibet, and passed them on, in secret, to his heart disciple Dromtönpa. Thus began the lineage of the great Kadampas, yogis famous for their practice of thought transformation. And these practices remain today the essential meditations of all Mahayana yogis.

Opening the Door of Dharma is in the tradition of these Kadampas. It emphasizes mainly the shortcomings of desire, and impermanence and death. These are "the first things to practice if you want to practice Dharma," because by recognizing that following desire is in fact the cause of suffering, not the cause of pleasure, and by meditating on death, one is able to begin to practice Dharma, and eventually to exchange oneself for others, to develop bodhicitta.

Here in *The Door to Satisfaction*, Lama Zopa Rinpoche shows, with clear and powerful reasoning, that by practicing these methods and by recognizing that there is no self to cherish, we can discover our deepest level of satisfaction and happiness, enlightenment, and perfectly lead others to this enlightened state.

This is Lama Zopa's heart advice and has been the essence of his teachings since he gave his first meditation course in 1971. Rinpoche is a modern day Kadampa; he is an impeccable example of the teachings he gives and constantly cherishes others more than himself.

Since his beloved Lama Yeshe passed away in 1984, Lama Zopa has been the sole Spiritual Director of the FPMT, which has grown to include, in seventeen countries, more than seventy centers for meditation, retreat, and healing, as well as monasteries, publishing houses, and other activities.

Kopan thrives. The Mount Everest Centre is now home to more than 250 monks and nuns, who study Buddhist philosophy in the traditional monastic way.

Rinpoche travels constantly between the various parts of his mandala, teaching and guiding his thousands of disciples. Special among those under Rinpoche's care is Lama Tenzin Ösel Rinpoche, a Spanish child born in 1985 who has been formally acknowledged by His Holiness the Dalai Lama as the reincarnation of Lama Thubten Yeshe. It is now Lama Zopa's turn to be "more than a father, more than a mother." Taking care of every moment of this young lama's upbringing and education, Lama Zopa is preparing him to carry on the immeasurable Dharma activities that he started as Lama Yeshe.

For their contributions to this book, we sincerely thank Merry Colony, Alfred Leyens, Connie Miller, Paula Chichester, and Roger Munro. May everyone who reads *The Door to Satisfaction* realize as quickly as possible their innate potential for the highest happiness.

1
Prologue

Like molding dough in your hand,
you can definitely turn your mind
whichever way you want.

Opening the Door of Dharma

*I*N 1974, WHILE I WAS STAYING in the cave of the previous Lawudo Lama in the Solu Khumbu region of Nepal, I decided to check through all the texts that had belonged to him. They were mostly Nyingma texts relating to the practices of various deities, but there was one text that is a fundamental practice of all four Tibetan sects. The text I found was *Opening the Door of Dharma: The Initial Stage of Training the Mind in the Graduated Path to Enlightenment.*

A collection of the advice of many Kadampa geshes, *Opening the Door of Dharma* is by Lodrö Gyaltsen, a disciple of both Lama Tsong Khapa and Khedrub Rinpoche, one of Lama Tsong Khapa's two spiritual sons. This text describes the initial stage of thought transformation, or mind training—in other words, the first thing to practice if you want to practice Dharma.

Only when I read this text did I come to know what the practice of Dharma really means. During all the years of my life up until then I had not known. Practicing Dharma is usually regarded as reading scriptures, studying, memorizing, debating, saying prayers, performing rituals, and so forth. It was only when I read this text that I found out how to practice Dharma. I was very shocked that all my past actions had not been Dharma. When I checked back, all those past years of memorizing and saying prayers were not Dharma. From all those years, nothing was Dharma.

I was born near Lawudo, in Thami, in 1946. When I was quite young, three or four years old, my mother sent me to a monastery near my home to learn the alphabet from my uncle, who was a monk in the Nyingma tradition. But this didn't last long. Because

I was very naughty, I escaped from the monastery many times and ran back to my mother's home. So my mother decided to send me away to a much more isolated place, called Rolwaling. Rolwaling is a secret holy place of Padmasambhava, where there are many wonderful, blessed caves.

Another uncle, Ngawang Gendun, took me from my home to Rolwaling. We had to cross very dangerous rocky mountains, with rocks falling down and water rushing past, then cross over snow for one or two days. While crossing the snow, we could see many deep crevasses going down hundreds of feet, with what looked like a sea at the bottom. It was a very, very hard journey.

I lived at Rolwaling for seven years, learning the alphabet again and then learning to read. My teacher was Ngawang Gendun, who at that time was also a monk. After learning to read the Tibetan letters, I spent the rest of the time memorizing prayers, as well as reading the *Kangyur* and *Tengyur* and doing pujas for people in their homes.

In Solu Khumbu, many lay people cannot even read the alphabet. The lamas usually allow them to come to initiations, but they can't take retreat commitments. The monks who are able to read and can understand the texts are given retreats to do, and the lay people are given a commitment to recite many millions of *om mani padme hungs* or some other mantra. Since these people cannot understand the texts, the lama gives them something that they can do.

These lay people are supposed to recite the mantras themselves, but often they go to the monks living nearby and ask them to help with the commitment. Offering a basket of potatoes, which is what they grow and eat, they come and say, "I received a commitment from this lama to do this many million mantras. Please do this many for me." Some people recite a few themselves then ask other people to do the rest.

So, I spent those seven years reading texts such as the *Kangyur*,

Tengyur, and *Prajnaparamita* in people's homes, when my uncle was asked to do pujas. Sometimes we would do a puja for someone who had died. In that region, the custom when someone dies is to have a special puja done and make large money offerings to the lamas and other people.

When I was about ten, I went to Tibet, to Domo Geshe Rinpoche's monastery near Pagri. I stayed there for three years. I spent the mornings memorizing texts and the rest of the day doing pujas in people's houses. I did my first examination there, with my manager making offerings to the monks. Pagri was a very active business center, where many traders came from Lhasa, Tsang, India—everywhere.

In March 1959, the Chinese took over Tibet, but because that area is close to India, there was no immediate danger. Later that year I was instructed to do my first retreat, on Lama Tsong Khapa Guru Yoga, at a nearby monastery called Pema Chöling, a branch of Domo Geshe's monastery. I didn't know anything about the meditation; I just recited the prayer and some *migtsemas*. I think I finished the retreat, but I don't know how I did it or how many mantras I counted.

At the end of 1959, when the threat of torture was imminent, we decided to escape to India. One day we heard that the Chinese would come to Pema Chöling in two days. That same night we very secretly left. We had to cross only one mountain to reach Bhutan. One night, because it was very wet and we could not see the road clearly, we had a little trouble, sinking into the mud and slipping over. There were nomads at the border. If they had seen us, it would have been difficult to escape because we had heard that some of them were spies, but even though their dogs were barking, the nomads did not come out of their tents.

5

Eventually we reached India. We went to Buxa Duar, in West Bengal, where the Indian Government housed the monks from Sera, Ganden, and Drepung monasteries who wanted to continue their studies. During the time of the British, Buxa was used as a concentration camp, with both Mahatma Gandhi and Nehru being imprisoned there. Where Mahatma Gandhi had been imprisoned became the nunnery, and where Nehru had been imprisoned became Sera Monastery's prayer hall.

My study of Buddhist philosophy began with Geshe Rabten Rinpoche teaching me *Collected Topics (Dura)*, the first debating subject. But Geshe Rabten had many disciples and was very busy, so one of his disciples, Gen Yeshe, who has since passed away, taught me. After that, I received teachings from Lama Yeshe.

While I was living at Buxa, because the conditions there were very poor, I caught TB. (Of course, that was not the only reason—there was karma as well!) Lama Yeshe and I then went to Darjeeling for nine months so that I could have medical treatment. It was at that time, in 1965, while we were staying at Domo Geshe's monastery in Darjeeling, that we met our first Western student, Zina Rachevsky. Zina's father had been a prince in Russia, but the family had escaped to France at the time of the Russian Revolution. Zina was born in France and later moved to America.

Zina asked us to go to live in Sri Lanka and to start a Dharma center there. We obtained permission to do this from His Holiness the Dalai Lama and from the Tibetan Government, but Zina had some problem that meant we could not go. Instead, since I was born in Nepal, we decided to visit Nepal.

We stayed in the Gelug monastery near Baudhanath Stupa, just outside Kathmandu. Every day Lama would look out through the window at a particular hill. He seemed very attracted to it, and one day we went out to check that hill. It was the Kopan hill.

6

During this time my mother and all my relatives came down from Solu Khumbu to Kathmandu on pilgrimage. Every twelve years there is a special occasion when all the Himalayan people come down from the mountains to go on pilgrimage to the holy places in the Kathmandu valley. They asked me to come back to Solu Khumbu, so I returned there.

It was at that time that Lawudo Cave was returned to me, and I began to build Lawudo Monastery. And Lama was gradually building Kopan Monastery then also. The two monasteries were being built at the same time. And it was then that I discovered Lodrö Gyaltsen's text.

TRANSFORMING THE MIND

Opening the Door of Dharma describes mainly impermanence and death, and the shortcomings of desire, the obstacles created by the eight worldly dharmas. These eight worldly concerns are:

(1) being happy when acquiring material things;
(2) being unhappy when not acquiring material things;
(3) wanting to be happy;
(4) not wanting to be unhappy;
(5) wanting to hear interesting sounds;
(6) not wanting to hear uninteresting sounds;
(7) wanting praise;
(8) not wanting criticism.

I don't know whether this text has been translated into English; it is not difficult to understand intellectually, but there are many old terms that need commentary.

Reading this text was very helpful. It showed me that, like molding dough in your hand, you can definitely turn your mind whichever way you want. It can be trained to turn this way, that way. Now my mind is completely degenerate, but at that time, having thought a little about the meaning of this text, I hated it when people came to make offerings to me.

After finding *Opening the Door of Dharma*, I did a deity retreat. I think because I understood from this text how to practice Dharma, even the very first day of retreat was unbelievably peaceful and joyful. Because of a slight weakening of the eight worldly dharmas, my mind was more tranquil and slightly purer. Like having fewer rocks blocking a road, there were fewer obstacles in my mind, which means less interference from the eight worldly dharmas. This is what makes a retreat successful. Even though I hadn't read carefully the commentaries of this tantric practice, the deity's blessing was received because of fewer problems in my mind.

Trying to control your mind clears away obstacles, and the pure Dharma that is in your mind brings you closer to the deity. Even though you may not be very familiar with the meditations, the blessings of the deity come. Experiencing good signs in the daytime during sessions and in the nighttime during dreams shows that the deity is pleased with you and is bestowing blessings. The success of a retreat seems basically to depend on this. It seems that receiving the blessings of a deity does not depend solely on knowing the meditations of the generation and completion stages of the tantric path.

(Of course, you may be unable to continue your retreat if the more you do retreat, the more *lung*, or wind, disease you develop. After meeting Tibetan Buddhism, you know all about lung! Before that, lung was not so famous. The main cause of lung, by the way, is the inability to practice the essence of this text, the real meaning of Dharma.)

As Kirti Tsenshab Rinpoche, holder of the entire holy Buddhadharma, has said, "All the teachings of the Buddha (Tibetan, *Kangyur*) and the commentaries by the pandits (*Tengyur*) are to subdue the mind." All of these teachings are mind training, thought transformation. All the teachings of Buddha are to transform the mind, to subdue the mind.

Opening the Door of Dharma is a thought transformation text, as I mentioned. Why is it called "thought transformation"? What is it that interferes with and renders ineffective our practice of listening to these teachings, reflecting on their meaning, and meditating on the path they reveal? The eight worldly dharmas, desire clinging to this life. The particular aim of this text is to control the eight worldly dharmas—this is thought transformation.

The whole teaching of the lam-rim, the graduated path to enlightenment, is thought transformation. Its main purpose is to subdue the mind. This is why listening to and reflecting and meditating on lam-rim teachings are so beneficial. When other teachings have no effect, hearing or reading the lam-rim can subdue your mind. The graduated path to enlightenment has a special arrangement that subdues the mind.

The lam-rim, as set out originally by Lama Atisha in his text, *Lamp on the Path to Enlightenment,* begins with the meditation on perfect human rebirth—the eight freedoms and ten richnesses. Lama Tsong Khapa, however, begins the lam-rim meditations with guru devotion, the root of the path.

Now, what blocks the generation of the graduated path to enlightenment within our mind? What doesn't allow us to have realizations, beginning with guru devotion or perfect human rebirth? Again, it is the eight worldly dharmas. Worldly concern does not allow the practice of lam-rim to become Dharma. What doesn't allow our everyday actions to become Dharma? From morning until night, what doesn't allow the actions we do to become holy Dharma? The eight worldly dharmas, desire clinging to this life. This is the obstacle that prevents the generation within our mind of the lam-rim from the very beginning up to enlightenment, that doesn't allow us to have realizations such as guru devotion or perfect human rebirth.

We need to train our mind by reflecting on the shortcomings of worldly concern and the infinite benefits of renouncing it. Especially we need to train our mind by meditating on impermanence and death. If this initial thought training is done, you open the door of Dharma. Then, without difficulty, you are able to practice Dharma. Every action you wish to do, whether retreat or other Dharma practices, you are able to do. And generally all your actions become Dharma. Not only that, you are able to begin to generate within your own mind the realizations of the path, from guru devotion or perfect human rebirth up to enlightenment. You are able to begin to generate the path to enlightenment within your mind, and to continue and complete it.

All these results come from this very first thought training, *Opening the Door of Dharma*. If you practice the meaning of this text, you will control the eight worldly dharmas instead of allowing yourself to be controlled by them. Instead of giving yourself no freedom, you will give yourself freedom. Otherwise you have no freedom, no independence.

2
Knowing How to Practice Dharma

Try to eliminate the negative attitudes,
which bring suffering, and increase
the positive attitudes, which bring happiness.

MOTIVATION

*M*OTIVATE THAT BY HEARING each word of this teaching you may be able to realize the whole path to enlightenment, especially bodhicitta. Pray for this to happen immediately, and for you to be able to cause this to happen also to all sentient beings. Pray that each word of this teaching subdues immediately the minds of other sentient beings. Pray that the whole path to enlightenment, especially bodhicitta, is generated in the minds of all sentient beings.

Hearing this teaching benefits your own mind, and later, because of having heard it, you will be able to benefit others. As you explain this teaching to others, each word will have much power because you previously made this motivation to benefit extensively other sentient beings. If you motivate like this now while you are listening to the teaching, in the future your own teaching will be able to subdue the minds of others very quickly and cause them to generate the path. This happens because of the power of the mind.

When you listen to the teachings, it is also very helpful to think that this is how all the Buddhas are guiding you. Meditating like this makes you feel a closer connection to the Buddhas. Think that all the Buddhas are teaching you, guiding you to the happiness of future lives, liberation, and enlightenment. Feel this in your heart. With this meditation, your own mind causes you to receive the blessings of all the Buddhas.

Think: "No matter how many eons it takes or how hard it is, I *must* achieve the state of omniscient mind, which is free of all obscurations and perfect in all realizations, for the sake of all mother sentient beings, who equal infinite space. Therefore, I'm going to clarify the righteous conduct of listening to the holy Dharma in accordance with the traditional practices of the lineage lamas."

In the short time that we are here in this greatest, most blessed, most precious holy place of Bodhgaya, where one thousand Buddhas will descend, we should take the opportunity to accumulate the most extensive merits possible. So, please listen well to the teaching.

TAKING THE ESSENCE OF THIS PRECIOUS HUMAN BODY

Opening the Door of Dharma begins with Lodrö Gyaltsen paying homage to the guru, Buddhas, bodhisattvas, and their entourages:

> May the teaching of the Buddha, origin of all sentient beings' benefits and happiness, flourish. I am requesting that it develop extensively. I am requesting that all sentient beings experience great bliss.

The title of the text is mentioned again, *Opening the Door of Dharma: The Initial Stage of Training the Mind in the Graduated Path to Enlightenment.* And then:

> I prostrate to the stainless lotus feet of the guru, who is inseparable from all the Buddhas and bodhisattvas of the ten directions, and take refuge in him.
>
> By paying homage to the lotus feet of the guru and relying upon him, I receive all perfections. To the guru-deity, I bow with respect and devotion.
>
> With compassion for those who seek to practice Dharma from the heart, I will reveal here how to practice the holy Dharma. I will reveal the teaching that enchants the learned ones adorned with the Buddha's teachings, as well as the commentaries written by the pandits and the guru's instructions. Listen respectfully and one-pointedly.

The guru to whom Lodrö Gyaltsen is prostrating is Khedrub

14

Rinpoche, one of Lama Tsong Khapa's heart disciples. Not only Lodrö Gyaltsen is paying homage to Khedrub Rinpoche, but so also are Brahma, Indra, and all beings of the three realms.

> From the holy mouth of the precious guru, essence of all the three times' Buddhas: "At this time that you have received a precious human body with freedom and richness, you must take the essence as much as possible. To do this, examine the difference between your mind and an animal's mind."

Examine an animal's mind. An animal thinks, "I want to be happy—I don't want to be cold, I don't want to be hungry." If you think of nothing other than that, you are no different from an animal. It is important to take the essence of this body, and in order to do that, you should not cling to this life.

The great bodhisattva Shantideva also says in *A Guide to the Bodhisattva's Way of Life*:

> This perfect human body, qualified by freedoms and richnesses, is extremely difficult to find. If one does not attempt to obtain the benefits of this human body now, how will one receive another in the future?

Asking how you will receive another perfect human rebirth in the future implies that, unless you attempt to obtain the benefit of this present human rebirth, you won't achieve another. And why do you need to obtain the benefit of this perfect human rebirth and get another? Because you do not want suffering and you do want happiness. It is not the case that you wish to have suffering and do not wish to have happiness. With this perfect human rebirth, we have the opportunity to create the causes to have happiness and avoid suffering.

Happiness and suffering come from your own mind, not from outside. Your own mind is the cause of happiness; your own mind is the cause of suffering. To obtain happiness and pacify suffering, you have to work within your own mind. The workshop is within your mind. You need to eliminate the mental factors, the thoughts, that bring suffering. You need to recognize and understand well those wrong ways of thinking, as well as the right ways of thinking that bring happiness. You do this by relying upon a correct teaching, such as the Buddhadharma. In the workshop of your own mind, by listening, reflecting, and meditating, you try to eliminate the negative attitudes, which bring suffering and to increase the positive attitudes, which bring happiness.

DISTINGUISHING BETWEEN VIRTUE AND NON-VIRTUE

At this time we have met the unmistaken Dharma, the teaching of the Buddha, particularly the teaching of the Mahayana, the Great Vehicle, which shows the path to great liberation, full enlightenment. We have met the Mahayana guru, and we have received a perfect human rebirth, the condition that allows us to put the teachings into practice.

From today, from this moment, we have a certain number of years, months, days, hours, minutes, seconds left to live. Each day, hour, minute, second is the time to decide where we will go after this life. Until we are liberated from samsara, cyclic existence, there are only two ways we can go after death: to the suffering migratory realms or the happy migratory realms. There is no third way. Each day, each hour, each minute, each second is the time to decide, to prepare. Until your death happens, each day, each hour, each minute, each second, you have the freedom to choose; you can decide to prevent rebirth as a suffering migratory being and to take rebirth as a happy migratory being. Each day, each minute is crucial, because each day, each minute, we are that much nearer to death. Think well, from the very depths of your heart. You have the opportunity to choose where to go, to prepare. Each moment of your life is very important, very precious.

As Nagarjuna says in *The Precious Garland*:

> Actions motivated by attachment, hatred, and ignorance are non-virtues. From these, all suffering migratory beings arise. From virtuous actions, all happy migratory beings arise, and in all lifetimes there will be happiness.

As Nagarjuna explains, everything—temporal and ultimate happiness, day-to-day problems and the endless future sufferings of samsara—is dependent upon your own mind, upon your own virtue and non-virtue.

Any action involves two motivations: the causal motivation and the motivation at the time. The causal motivation is the original motivation for doing anything, the first thought that comes into your mind to do something: the initial action, karma, of the mind. The thought in your mind while you are doing the action of body or speech that you initially motivated to do is the motivation at the time: the subsequent action of the mind.

So, karma is related to thought. The body of the happy transmigrator (god or human being) and the body of the unhappy transmigrator (hell, *preta*, or animal being) are creations of your own mind; these bodies are created by your way of thinking, by your motivation, mainly the causal motivation.

Until you achieve the patience level of the path of preparation, you cannot have definite confidence that you will not be reborn in the lower realms. When you achieve this path, however, you can have complete confidence that you will not be reborn there. When you achieve the path of seeing, you are beyond craving, so you do not create new negative karma, new causes of samsara.

Until you achieve the cessation of all disturbing-thought obscurations, there are only two ways to reincarnate after death: lower realms or upper realms. Which way you go is determined by karma, the action of your mind, your motivation.

Lama Atisha's heart-son Dromtönpa asked, "What is the result of actions done out of worldly concern?" Lama Atisha replied, "The result will be only itself." I think "only itself" means only suffering. To make the answer clear, Dromtönpa asked the question again, this time asking what the result would be in future lives. Lama Atisha replied, "Hell, preta, animal!" This means that any action done with the thought of worldly concern, clinging to this life, is non-virtuous.

Generally, ten non-virtues are given as the examples of negative karmas that have the ripening result of rebirth in the lower realms: killing, stealing, sexual misconduct, lying, slander, harsh speech, gossip, covetousness, ill will, and wrong views. And, for example, a fully ordained monk has various categories of negative karma, which include defeat, downfall, and individual confession. In his lam-rim teachings *Liberation in the Palm of Your Hand*, Pabongka Dechen Nyingpo says that a defeat results in rebirth in the unbearable suffering state of the hot hells; a downfall, rebirth in the Black-Line Hell; the lightest category of individual confession, rebirth in the Reviving Hell.

When we do purification practices, such as Vajrasattva meditation or prostrations, as well as feeling regret for having created particular non-virtues, it is important to remember this definition of non-virtue: that all actions done out of worldly concern, clinging to this life, are non-virtues. By remembering this broad definition of how an action becomes a non-virtue, we have an extensive view of the negative karma that needs to be purified; otherwise, what we regret will be very limited. And do not think only of this life but of beginningless rebirths.

Even though we may think we are practicing Dharma, either

18

we have no motivation or our motivation is very weak, and our practice is not done perfectly. We may recite mantras, but our minds are distracted and we have no concentration, so the virtue is weak. At the end of our practice, we do not dedicate the virtue that has been accumulated, or we dedicate with pride, which weakens the virtue. Or even if the virtue is dedicated to achieve enlightenment, anger and heresy destroy the merit and delay the experience of the resultant realizations for many eons.

We create very little virtue, good karma, and even when we do create some virtue, it is not perfect. But we create powerful negative karmas. If death happened right now, we would definitely be reborn in the lower realms. And if we are reborn there, we will have no opportunity to practice Dharma, even for our own future-life happiness and liberation. There will be no opportunity to practice Dharma for ourselves and no opportunity to practice for others. We will be completely overwhelmed by suffering and again create negative karma. Like this, dying and being reborn in the lower realms, we will wander for an incredible length of time.

It is not just that we are nearer to death as each second passes; we are nearer to the hot and cold hells. Before, I mentioned being nearer to death; but it's more than that—we are constantly nearer to the lower realms.

THREE LEVELS OF HAPPINESS

If you understand lam-rim, the graduated path to enlightenment, you know the benefits you can receive from this perfect human body. The first is happiness of future lives, which means receiving the body of a happy migratory being, such as a god or human. The second benefit is liberation from samsara, release forever from the bondage of karma and delusion. The third is attainment of the non-abiding sorrowless state, full enlightenment, the cessation of the two types of obscuration: the disturbing-thought obscurations and the obscurations to omniscience. It is these three benefits, or levels of happiness, that Shantideva refers to in the verse I mentioned earlier and that he means we should obtain with this present perfect human rebirth.

In order to receive these three benefits, we need to follow the graduated paths of the three levels of capability, of the three capable beings. The first, the graduated path of lower capability, is described in the following way by Lama Atisha in *Lamp on the Path to Enlightenment.* He says that if the motivation is to cut off clinging to this life completely and achieve the body of a happy transmigratory being in the next life, one should, with the realization of the shortcomings of non-virtuous actions, renounce the ten non-virtues and practice the ten virtues. This person, who protects karma and lives in morality with the aim to receive just the happiness of future lives, is a lower capable being.

With the second, the path of middle capability, one sees that the entire samsara—these aggregates caused by karma and delusion—is only suffering. Because they are contaminated by the seed of delusions, these aggregates again cause the future-life samsara. Seeing samsara as complete suffering, like being in the center of a fire, one turns one's back on it, fully renouncing it. There is not the slightest attraction to samsara, to samsaric perfections. The aim of middle capable beings is to achieve their own liberation from samsara, from the bondage of karma and delusion, and the method to achieve this is the practice of the path of the three higher trainings: morality, concentration, and wisdom.

Now the third, the person of higher capability, completely renounces cherishing the self and instead cherishes other sentient beings, with the aim to achieve full enlightenment for their sake. The method to achieve this is practice of the path of the causal vehicle, Paramitayana, in which one practices the six *paramitas,* or perfections, of a bodhisattva (giving, patience, morality, enthusiastic perseverance, concentration, and wisdom). On the basis of this, the person of higher capability, a great capable being, also practices the resultant vehicle, Vajrayana.

Practicing the graduated path of higher capability depends on practicing the graduated path of middle capability, which means, in general, having the attitude of renouncing the whole of samsara and practicing the three higher trainings. Practicing the path of middle capability, in turn, is dependent upon practicing the graduated path of lower capability, which means, in general, having the attitude of cutting off clinging to this life and practicing morality, such as the ten virtues. The term *in general* is used because the attitude and practice of the first path is the foundation for the second and third paths, and the second path is the foundation for the third.

Opening the Door of Dharma also describes these three paths in the following way:

> Anyone who performs Dharma or worldly activities with desire for the body of a god or human in the next life is called a lower capable being. All actions done with that motivation are the cause only of samsara.
>
> Anyone who wishes to be liberated from samsara and practices Dharma with aversion to all samsaric activities is called a middle capable being. All such actions are virtuous and are the cause only of liberation from samsara.
>
> Anyone whose actions are done not just to achieve self-liberation but for the liberation of all sentient beings is called a great, or supreme, capable being. These actions are the cause of achieving enlightenment.
>
> These three beings are distinguished only according to the mind.

A capable being has to be one of the three types I have just described. We have to examine our own mind to see whether we are in any of these lineages. If we are not, we should attempt to enter them.

ANIMAL IN A HUMAN MASK

Now, as Panchen Lama Losang Chökyi Gyaltsen explains in his commentary on Lama Atisha's *Lamp on the Path to Enlightenment*:

> Those who live their lives with the aim to obtain only the happiness of this life are not actually capable beings—they are ordinary beings.

Creatures such as mice and mosquitoes have nothing to think about other than the pleasure of this life, and all their actions are done seeking this. So they are ordinary beings. What they do is nothing special, and it's done just for this life. Having a human body, especially a perfect human body, we should try, from morning until night, not to be ordinary beings like these dumb animals. During the whole twenty-four hours, when we sleep, eat, drink, walk, sit, and so on, we should attempt to be better than this. Our actions should not be like theirs. In other words, we should not live our lives in the same way as non-human beings that have not received a precious human birth.

Achieving this depends on our attitude. We have to constantly watch our mind, using our mind as the object of concentration. We have to be a spy, watching our own mind. This gives us freedom, allowing us to recognize our wrong ways of thinking, or non-virtuous motivations, and right ways of thinking, or virtuous motivations. Recognizing our attitudes gives us freedom to transform our mind from non-virtue into virtue. In this way our life becomes superior to an animal's, and we fulfill the purpose of being a human being. Our life becomes meaningful. Otherwise, like a performer wearing the mask and costume of a deity in a religious dance, we are wearing a human mask while inside we are an animal. We are an animal in a human mask.

In *A Guide to the Bodhisattva's Way of Life*, the great bodhisattva Shantideva says:

> Having received this freedom once, if I don't train in virtue now, what will I do when I am born in an evil-gone realm, ignorant and constantly suffering?

Having just once this precious human body, qualified by the eight freedoms and ten richnesses, is like a dream; it's like a beggar finding a million dollars in a garbage can.

Shantideva clearly says that if we don't train our mind in virtue, we will be born in the evil-gone realms, or *ngen-song*. *Ngen* means evil, which refers to negative karma; *song* means gone. The connotation here is that, because of negative karma, one is gone; that is, the consciousness migrates to the body of an animal, preta, or hell being.

If one is born in the body of a dog, a pig, or a worm, for example, one is so ignorant that there is no freedom to understand even the definitions of virtue and non-virtue. Even if someone were to explain these definitions into an animal's ear for hundreds of eons, there would be no way it could understand the meaning. This is why Shantideva says, "When I'm born in an evil-gone realm, ignorant and constantly suffering, what can I do then?" At that time there is nothing we can do; we are finished. So, before being born in those unfortunate realms, we would be wise to hurry up and practice Dharma.

Having this precious body that gives you the freedom to train your mind in virtue, in Dharma, you can accumulate many virtues, but the main virtue you should concentrate on is training your mind in the graduated paths to enlightenment of the three levels of capability. The main point is to train your mind in the lam-rim.

23

MEDITATION ON THE LAM-RIM

In his lam-rim teachings, Pabongka Dechen Nyingpo explains that it is very good to do direct meditation on the lam-rim—even on a simple lam-rim prayer such as Lama Tsong Khapa's *Foundation of All Good Qualities*. Direct meditation means that we recite the lam-rim prayer, being mindful of its meaning; in that way, the practice becomes a direct meditation on the whole path to enlightenment. This meditation is much more important than reciting many millions of mantras or even meeting Buddha. This is understandable. Why? When doing retreat, why do we meditate on guru yoga, seeing the guru as inseparable from the deity? Why do we meditate on deities and recite so many mantras? To help us complete the lam-rim path. Without actualizing the three principal aspects of the path to enlightenment (renunciation, bodhicitta, emptiness), we cannot complete the tantric path. We may have some experiences up to a certain level, but we cannot complete the path.

Without realizing emptiness, for example, there is no way to achieve clear light, the illusory body, or the unification of no more learning, which involves the completely pure holy body and holy mind. Also, without at least creative bodhicitta, even meditations such as inner fire do not become the cause of enlightenment. Without the actual realization of bodhicitta, there is no way to experience the completion stage clear light and illusory body. To achieve clear light, which is the cause of *dharmakaya*, and the illusory body, cause of *rupakaya*, one needs to accumulate infinite merit. The cause of the infinite merit needed so that one can actualize clear light and the illusory body is bodhicitta.

When doing deity retreats, we recite each mantra in order to make it possible to have lam-rim realizations within our mind. We do guru yoga practice in order to receive blessings to be able to actualize the lam-rim within our mind. Everything is done for this reason.

24

Unless the three principal aspects of the path are realized within our mind, there is no way to achieve enlightenment, to complete the tantric path. Even though one may have recited many millions of mantras or even seen Buddha, unless one has actualized the three principal aspects of the path, there is no way to achieve enlightenment. What Pabongka Dechen Nyingpo is saying makes sense. To complete the tantric path, one has to train the mind in the common path, the three principal aspects of the path, the lam-rim; there is no way to skip that.

Direct meditation on lam-rim even once is much more precious than other practices because it leaves the imprint of the whole path to enlightenment on our mental continuum, making it possible sooner or later to actualize the whole path. This is what really brings us to enlightenment. If we leave out meditation on the lam-rim, no matter how many retreats or other practices we do, we will not find any change in our mind. Even after reciting millions of mantras, with our fingers and malas completely worn, our mind will still be at the same level.

Why doesn't anything happen? Why isn't there any change in the mind? Why aren't there any realizations? Our mind stays at the same level—or becomes even worse!—because we don't actually train our mind in the lam-rim, in each step of the graduated path to enlightenment. There is a danger of leaving out this main practice, of ignoring the main trunk of the tree and instead seeking the branches.

In the West there are many competitions: car racing, horse racing, running, walking. Here, seeking the happiness of future lives, liberation, and enlightenment, we should have a competition between our Dharma practice and our life. Or at the very least we should try to make them equal. As our life passes— minute by minute, hour by hour, day by day—we should be practicing Dharma, making our life equal to Dharma. As His

Holiness the Dalai Lama often says, "If one cannot make the whole day become Dharma, try to make at least half the day become Dharma." (And this doesn't mean you practice Dharma until noon, then don't practice after that!)

3

Giving Up This Life

Lama Atisha replied, "Give up this life in your mind!"

LAMA ATISHA

*L*AMA ATISHA, WHO WROTE the first lam-rim text, *Lamp on the Path to Enlightenment,* was a great pandit with infinite knowledge and realizations who helped to spread the Dharma extensively. Accomplished in the five types of knowledge, he actualized single-pointed concentration and clairvoyance and was guided by many deities. He built many temples and monasteries in India, Tibet and Nepal. He lived a total of seventy-two years, from 982 to 1054, seventeen of them in Tibet.

Through Lama Atisha's kindness in writing *Lamp on the Path to Enlightenment,* those of us who have met the lam-rim do not have any confusion now about where to begin the graduated path to enlightenment. Those who haven't met the lam-rim don't know where to begin. Even though a person may have studied many sutras and other texts, if you ask them, "How do you begin the path?" they don't know how to answer; and if they do answer, the answer is back to front, with later practices mentioned before the earlier steps of the path.

We are extremely fortunate that Lama Atisha, in *Lamp on the Path to Enlightenment,* integrated the entire sutra and tantra paths of Buddha—Hinayana, Paramitayana, and Tantrayana—setting up the whole path as a graduated practice by which one can achieve enlightenment. From the side of the teachings, everything is very clear; the only problem is that we don't practice.

Lama Atisha had many great disciples: the main ones in India were the pandit Bhumisara and King Mahapali; and in Tibet, in addition to his heart disciple Dromtönpa, three Kadampa geshes: Gönpawa, Naljor Chaktri Chok, and Jangchub Rinchen. There were also many other disciples, such as King Yeshe Öd's nephew, Jangchub Öd; Rinchen Zangpo; and Lotsawa Nagtso. Even the disciples of Lama Atisha had infinite qualities, which are explained in their biographies.

When Lama Atisha was about to pass away, Geshe Naljor Chaktri Chok said to him, "After you have passed away, I will dedicate myself to meditation." Lama Atisha answered, "Give up anything that is a bad action!" Lama Atisha did not say that it was good to meditate; he did not say, "Oh yes, that is very good!" Instead he said, "Give up anything that is a bad action!"

Naljor Chaktri Chok then said to Lama Atisha, "In that case, sometimes I will explain Dharma and sometimes meditate." Again Lama Atisha gave the same answer. Naljor Chaktri Chok thought some more, then gave another suggestion. But no matter what he said, Lama Atisha just kept on giving the same answer. Finally, Naljor Chaktri Chok asked, "Well, what should I do?" Lama Atisha replied, "Give up this life in your mind!"

Keeping this advice in his heart, Naljor Chaktri Chok lived in a juniper forest near Reting Monastery, no different from the way animals live in a forest. This is not talking about his mind—just his body. Living alone, not seeing even one other human face, he passed his life there.

DROMTÖNPA

Dromtönpa, Lama Atisha's translator, was born to the north of Lhasa, quite near to Tölung, where Lama Yeshe was born. This is the holy place where Lama Tsong Khapa saw Guhyasamaja and Mahakala. I gave a Chenrezig initiation there during a pilgrimage to Tibet in 1987. This is also the place where Lower Tantric College monks took examinations, received commentaries on tantric root texts from their abbot, and practiced chanting. It seems that, quite close to here, Dromtönpa was born.

Tara prophesied the birth of Dromtönpa, who was an embodiment of Chenrezig. Tara predicted that Dromtönpa would be a holder of the Buddhadharma whose holy mind would be enriched with infinite qualities of scriptural understanding and realizations and who would see inconceivable numbers of deities.

Before coming to Central Tibet and becoming Lama Atisha's translator, Dromtönpa lived in Kham and was the disciple-servant of Lama Setsuen. After meeting Lama Atisha, Dromtönpa asked him what had been the best Dharma practice out of all the things he, Dromtönpa, had done. He told Lama Atisha about his various practices. He also explained how hard he had worked for Lama Setsuen. At night, armed, he guarded all the lama's animals. During the daytime, he did many other things. He made all the fires. The lama's wife used Dromtönpa as a chair to sit on while she milked the cows. While Dromtönpa was using his hands to spin yarn, his feet would be working butter into dried animal skins to make them pliable. At the same time, he would also be carrying something on his back. For many years, he worked like this—doing many things at the same time. Dromtönpa explained all this to Lama Atisha, who said, "Of all the things you have done, your hard work for Lama Setsuen has been the real Dharma."

Dromtönpa devoted himself correctly to Lama Atisha for seventeen years. After Dromtönpa met Lama Atisha, he never left Lama Atisha in the dark at night: every night he offered a butter lamp in Lama Atisha's room.

The lineage of the Kadampa geshes actually starts with Dromtönpa. Amongst his many disciples, Dromtönpa had three great sons, or chief disciples—Geshe Potowa, Geshe Chen-ngawa, and Geshe Puchungwa—who were holders of the Buddhadharma, with infinite realizations. After he established Reting Monastery in 1057, Dromtönpa lived another seven years, living a total of fifty-one years.

Dromtönpa was not a monk but a lay person living in the five precepts. When visualizing the lineage lamas of the lam-rim, you visualize Dromtönpa as a Tibetan nomad wearing a very warm, blue *chuba* lined with animal skin.

Dromtönpa always wore very old, torn clothes. Throwing the sleeves of his chuba over his shoulders, he would sometimes go off into the juniper forest. By putting two or three poles together and covering them with animal-hair cloth as Tibetan nomads do, Dromtönpa would make a small shelter and meditate inside.

While walking through the forest, Dromtönpa would sometimes recite this verse from Nagarjuna's *Letter to a Friend*:

> Acquiring things, not acquiring things; comfort, discomfort; interesting sounds, uninteresting sounds; praise, criticism: these eight worldly dharmas are not objects of my mind. They are all the same to me.

He would also recite from *A Guide to the Bodhisattva's Way of Life*, saying: "I am a seeker of liberation. I don't need to be bound by the receiving of material and respect." Sometimes he would recite the complete quote; at other times he would just begin the quotation. While he was reciting this he would shake his head, indicating that he didn't need to be bound by receiving material and respect.

Other Kadampa geshes would say, "For himself, Dromtönpa doesn't need to lead an ascetic life; he does this for the disciples who follow him."

Dromtönpa, who had abandoned all worldly activities, was once invited to a place called Rong to give money offerings to the monks during puja. He called one of his disciples, Pelgye Wangchuk, and said to him, "You go this time—I can't. I am here trying to give up this life."

~:ॐ:~

Seeing a monk circumambulating a monastery one day, Drom-tönpa called to him, "It is good to circumambulate, but it would be better to practice Dharma." The monk thought, "Maybe it's better to do prostrations."

When he saw the monk prostrating, Dromtönpa said to him, "It is good that you are doing prostrations, but it would be better to practice Dharma." When the monk tried reciting prayers and meditating, Dromtönpa again said the same thing.

Finally the monk asked Dromtönpa, "Then, what *should* I do?" Dromtönpa answered, "Give up this life in your mind!" Dromtönpa said this three times to the monk, "Give up this life in your mind! Give up this life in your mind!"

4

Transforming Non-Virtue into Virtue

Everything has to do with your own attitude,
your own way of thinking, your motivation.

HAVING A PURE MOTIVATION

*N*O MATTER WHAT ACTION you do, it is extremely important to have the right motivation. Whether you are a farmer or a meditator, if you act out of desire for this life's comfort and reputation, you are no different from an animal.

When I asked one abbot what worldly dharma means, he replied that it means gambling, working in the fields, and so on—that these are worldly activities. It is very common to think of worldly actions in this way, relating just to the action and not to the motivation, the attitude. If done with a pure motivation, however, actions such as gambling or working in the fields can become pure Dharma.

By itself, no action can be defined as a worldly action. It could be holy Dharma or worldly dharma, virtuous or non-virtuous—it could be anything. Only by knowing their motivation can you label people's actions holy Dharma or worldly dharma, whether it is farm work or meditation practice.

In *Liberation in the Palm of Your Hand,* Pabongka Dechen Nyingpo gives the following example: Four people are reciting praises to Tara. The first person recites the prayer with the motivation to achieve enlightenment for the sake of other sentient beings; the second, with the motivation to achieve liberation for the self; the third, to achieve happiness in future lives; and the fourth, seeking happiness only in this life.

The first person's action of reciting the prayer becomes the cause of enlightenment. The second person's action does not become the cause of enlightenment as it is done with the motivation to achieve self-liberation. This action becomes the cause of just that, liberation, which means release from samsara; it is not the cause of enlightenment, which is the mental state free of all mistakes and perfect in all qualities, all realizations.

The third person's recitation becomes the cause of achieving neither full enlightenment nor liberation. Since the action is done with the motivation to achieve only the happiness of future lives, it becomes the cause to achieve only samsaric happiness, with rebirth as a god or human being.

The recitations of these three people are all actions of holy Dharma. The fourth person's recitation, however, is not holy Dharma; it is worldly dharma because the action is done with worldly concern, clinging to this life. That motivation is non-virtuous. As I mentioned earlier, actions done out of worldly concern, attachment clinging just to the happiness of this life, are non-virtuous and result in rebirth in the hell, preta, or animal realms. So, even though the prayer itself is Dharma, the person's action does not become holy Dharma.

Pabongka Dechen Nyingpo uses the action of reciting a prayer as his example in order to clarify a common mistake. It is very easy to think that because a person's action is related to Dharma—reciting a prayer, reading a Dharma text, meditating—it is a Dharma action. It is very easy to believe this.

If the action of reciting a prayer with worldly concern could bring success, if it could become the cause of happiness, then robbing banks could also be a cause of happiness. By robbing banks, a person could become wealthy and live in comfort. So, does stealing really cause happiness? There is some similarity between the two examples. If that non-virtuous action of stealing done out of self-cherishing, attachment, anger, or some other delusion were the cause of happiness, then you could experience happiness from non-virtue. This mistaken idea would naturally follow.

Only actions that are not motivated by worldly concern, that are remedies for worldly concern, become Dharma. From morning until night, whatever actions we do—sleeping, eating, sitting, walking, talking—if done as remedies for delusions, become

Dharma. Actions done out of worldly concern, attachment to this life, however, become worldly dharma, or non-virtue. They do not become holy Dharma.

As the great bodhisattva Shantideva says in *A Guide to the Bodhisattva's Way of Life*:

> Though wishing to achieve happiness and to cease suffering, not knowing the secret of the mind, the supreme meaning of Dharma, beings wander meaninglessly.

Here, "the secret of the mind" does not mean some high realization such as clear light or the illusory body or their unification; it is not talking about anything very complicated. We can interpret "the secret of the mind" as meaning these different levels of motivation. This verse emphasizes the importance of watching and protecting our mind, keeping it in virtue, because happiness and suffering are dependent upon our own mind, our own good and bad thoughts. One way of thinking creates happiness; another way of thinking produces sufferings and problems. Everything—from day-to-day problems and the sufferings of the six realms up to liberation and enlightenment—depends on our mind, our way of thinking.

You may not be aware of this secret of the mind, that all your happiness and suffering come from your own mind: your way of thinking and your attitude. By knowing this secret, you can eliminate the wrong ways of thinking that produce your problems and all the sufferings of your future lives, all the obstacles to achieving enlightenment. With the correct way of thinking, you are able to obtain any happiness you wish.

THE TWO BEGGARS

Another quotation from *Opening the Door of Dharma* says:

> Before Dharma activities, the function of the mind

[which means the motivation] is the most important.
If one talks or works with a negative mind, one
receives suffering from that action, as in the example
of the head cut off by the wheel. If one talks or works
with a calm mind, one will receive happiness from
that action, as in the example of the moving shadow.

This means that one receives suffering from actions done with
the three poisonous minds.

The examples mentioned relate to the following story, as told
by His Holiness Song Rinpoche. Two beggars went separately to
beg food from a monastery. One went in the evening when the
monks were fasting, so he didn't get any food. The other beggar
went at the right time, when the monks were having lunch, so he
received plenty.

The beggar who didn't receive any food got very angry. Out of
anger, he said, "I wish I could cut off the heads of all the monks
and watch them drop on the ground!" Very soon after he had
said this, he was lying down by the side of a road when a chariot
came past, and one of its wheels cut off his head.

The other beggar who got plenty of food was very happy.
Feeling grateful to the monks, he said, "I wish I could offer the
monks nectar of the gods!" This wish generated enormous merit
in his mind. Afterwards he went to lie in a park under a tree,
where he stayed for the rest of the day. Throughout the whole
time, the shade of the tree did not move away from him. At that
time the local people were searching for someone with special
qualities to be their new king. Seeing the beggar who was always
covered by the shade of the tree, they asked him to be their leader.

There are three types of karma (in terms of when it ripens):
karma that you create and experience the result of in this life;
karma that you create in this life but experience the result of in
the next life; and karma that you create in this life but experience

the result of only after many lifetimes. Even though the beggar did not actually offer nectar to the monks, since the Sangha are a very powerful object because of the number of vows they hold, merely by having the wish to offer them nectar, he accumulated great merit. For this reason, the result of that karma was experienced in the same life.

THE BODHISATTVA CAPTAIN

There are also other stories. Generally, killing is negative karma. However, in one of his past lives, Guru Shakyamuni Buddha killed a human being. He was the captain of a ship that was carrying five hundred traders, and one person on board was planning to kill all the others. Realizing this and thinking that the person would go to hell and experience suffering for many eons if he succeeded in his plan, the captain felt unbearable compassion for him. He thought, "I will go to hell in his place. I will kill him before he has the chance to kill the others. Even if the karma of killing him means that I have to go to hell, I'll still do it." So, out of unbearable compassion, the captain killed the trader.

However, because of the motivation of great compassion, this action of killing did not become negative karma; instead, it became a special means of accumulating merit and shortened his stay in samsara by 100,000 eons. The text says very clearly here that this action did not become negative karma, though sometimes this is disputed. Some people find it very difficult to accept that this action of killing done out of compassion is virtuous. They argue that the motivation is virtuous but the action itself is non-virtuous, so the bodhisattva captain would have to experience some negative result because of that. Some geshes may argue like this in the context of Hinayana teachings, but it says very clearly here, in this Paramitayana text, that the captain's action was not negative karma.

In the Hinayana teachings, it is fixed that the three actions of body (killing, stealing, sexual misconduct) and the four actions of speech (lying, slandering, gossiping, speaking harshly) are negative. There is no permission given to perform these actions because Hinayana teachings emphasize the action more than the attitude. However, in the Paramitayana teachings, Buddha permitted these actions when a bodhisattva sees that the action will definitely bring great benefit to sentient beings. Buddha permitted this because there is no danger to the bodhisattva in terms of the development of his mind. His action does not become an obstacle to the achievement of enlightenment; instead, it actually helps the bodhisattva to achieve enlightenment more quickly. When there is great benefit, and especially when there is no danger, Buddha permitted such actions.

Hinayana is the foundation of Paramitayana, but Hinayana teachings do not mention bodhicitta, which is revealed in the Paramitayana. In Paramitayana, the mind of bodhicitta can make non-virtuous actions virtuous. In developing the mind, you first transform the indifferent mind into virtue; then, by generating bodhicitta and gradually developing it, after some time you are advanced enough to be able to transform even non-virtue into virtue. Bodhicitta enables us to do this.

In *Liberation in the Palm of Your Hand,* Pabongka Dechen Nyingpo explains that the captain's action of killing "accumulated much merit"; but here in the text, this is clarified even further: "This action of killing did not become negative karma and, on top of that, became a special method for completing the merit and so forth." Many other teachings agree with this, and even from a worldly point of view, it makes sense.

The text also says:

> If you give food and drink in order to tease someone
> or to cause a problem, unhappiness comes instead of
> happiness.

42

In other words, you give food and drink to someone with the motivation to harm them, to cause trouble. Here, even though the action may look very nice, the results will actually be negative—unhappiness in this life and suffering in future lives—because the motivation is negative. This is the opposite to the example of the bodhisattva captain, whose action of killing did not become negative karma but instead became a means to accumulate merit.

The text continues:

> If one gives with devotion, respect, compassion, and so forth, there is great joy from one's own side, and from the side of others. Great joy also results from that karma later. Therefore, everything is dependent on the mind. Happiness, suffering, negative karma, positive karma: everything has to do with different minds.

In other words, everything has to do with your own attitude, your own way of thinking, your motivation. Lama Tsong Khapa says in one of his lam-rim teachings that, apart from some exceptional actions, unless an action is motivated by one of the three principal aspects of the path, it becomes a cause of samsara, a cause of suffering. The exceptional actions that do not depend on motivation are those done in relation to holy objects such as Buddha, Dharma, Sangha. Making offerings to these holy objects, even with the motivation of worldly concern, results in happiness.

A sutra says: "The world is led by the mind." This means that the mind is the producer, or creator, of the world. All happiness, for example, is led by the virtuous mind. All the good things—the body of a god or human, the good places, desirable sense objects—arise in dependence upon the virtuous mind. By practicing bodhicitta, one is able to generate all the rest of the Mahayana path, tantric realizations, and enlightenment. All these come from, or are led by, bodhicitta.

All suffering is led by the non-virtuous mind. All the bad things—the bodies of the suffering transmigratory beings, the lower realms—arise in dependence upon the non-virtuous mind.

Everything comes from the mind, but the mind is formless. The sutra then says: "The mind does not see the mind." I think this means that, because the mind does not have color or shape, we cannot see or feel it in the way we can see and feel our body and other objects. Our mind and our delusions are formless and color-less. However, our ignorance believing in true existence is harder than a rocky mountain. Our delusions are harder than steel.

Rocky mountains and steel have a beginning and an end; they can be destroyed by external factors, such as the fire at the end of the eon or the heat of seven suns. However, the continuity of our delusions, our ignorance, does not have a beginning. Our igno-rance is beginningless, yet it still hasn't changed. This is amazing. And unless we train our mind and actualize the path, our delu-sions have no end. If we are able to generate the remedy of the path, we can end the delusions.

The quotation from the sutra finishes: "Whether an action is virtue or non-virtue, it is collected by the mind."

TRANSFORMING NON-VIRTUE INTO VIRTUE

Aryadeva tells the story of an *arhat* who was in great pain and asked another monk, his disciple, to suffocate him. So the disci-ple suffocated the arhat. This disciple then asked Guru Shakyamuni Buddha about the karma of his action. Buddha said that since the action was done with a good motivation, it did not create the karma of killing an arhat, which is one of the five uninterrupted negative karmas. Because the action was done with a good heart, as the arhat was in much pain, Buddha said it did not become an uninterrupted negative karma, only virtue.

However, there is another aspect to consider in the killing of beings to relieve their suffering. If a person or animal is going to be reborn in hell, since the suffering here in the human realm is nothing compared to that, it may be better for them to have one day longer here where the suffering is less. If the being is going to be reborn in the higher realms, as a god or human being, it is just a question of changing the body. This requires thorough checking. In fact, we need clairvoyance to make a decision like this.

Killing such beings may become virtuous because it is done with a good heart; but thinking about the nature of the being's future life, whether it will be in a lower or higher realm, makes a difference from the side of the other being. This is why *Lamp on the Path to Enlightenment* says that it is difficult to work for other sentient beings without clairvoyance.

There is another story of an old monk who had a son who was also a monk in the same monastery. One day the temple bell rang to call all the monks to confession. Hearing this, the young monk told his father to hurry up. By going quickly, the old monk died. When the young monk checked with Buddha, Buddha said that because the action was done with a good heart, it did not become the uninterrupted negative karma of killing one's father.

Aryadeva also gives another example: Someone saw a statue of Buddha sitting out in the rain, so he put his shoes on the head of the statue to protect it. After the rain stopped, somebody else came along and said, "Oh, how terrible it is to put shoes on a statue of Buddha!" and removed them. Both of these people created the cause to be born as Wheel-turning Kings. Why? Because both actions were done with good motivation. Both the one who put his shoes on the Buddha statue to protect it from the rain and the other who removed them created good karma.

The motivation is the essential thing, especially the causal motivation, as I mentioned earlier. If possible the motivation at the time should also be virtuous, but of the two, the causal motivation is more important. Apart from those exceptional actions I have already mentioned—actions done in relation to Buddha, Dharma, Sangha—it is the causal motivation that determines whether an action becomes virtue or non-virtue.

This is written particularly clearly here in *Opening the Door of Dharma*. I will repeat it again:

> For most people, killing is negative karma. However, because the action of the captain who killed a human being was motivated by great compassion, it did not become negative karma. On top of that, it became a special method of completing the merit and so forth.

An enormous amount of merit was accumulated because the captain sacrificed himself completely, happy to be reborn in hell by killing the man and thus saving him from hell.

It is said many times in the teachings that bodhicitta is a special method of accumulating merit. This is also very clearly explained in the extensive thought-training teachings of Kachen Yeshe Gyaltsen. So, one can transform non-virtue into virtue. It's all a question of motivation.

5
Cutting Off Desire

Less desire means less pain.

DESIRE IS SUFFERING

*N*OT FOLLOWING DESIRE is practicing Dharma; following desire is not practicing Dharma. It is as simple as that. The whole point of *Opening the Door of Dharma*, these instructions from the holy mouths of the Kadampa geshes, which they practiced and experienced, is to cut off the eight worldly dharmas, to be free of desire clinging to this life. Whether you are practicing Dharma or not, the evil thought of the eight worldly dharmas is the source of all obstacles and problems. Everything undesirable comes from this thought of the worldly dharmas.

When you are told that you have to give up desire, you feel as if you are being told to sacrifice your happiness. You give up desire, then you don't have happiness and you're left with nothing. Just yourself. Your desire has been confiscated; you have been robbed of your happiness; and you are left there empty, like a deflated balloon. You feel as if you no longer have a heart in your body, as if you have lost your life.

This is because you have not realized the shortcomings of desire. You have not recognized that the nature of desire is suffering. Desire itself is a suffering, unhealthy mind. Because of desire, the mind hallucinates, and you are unable to see that there is another happiness, real happiness.

For example, when there is desire for an object and enjoyment of it, you label this experience "happiness." It appears to you as happiness, but in reality it is only suffering. As you keep doing the action, such as eating food, your happiness doesn't increase but only decreases. As your stomach becomes full, your happiness then becomes the suffering of suffering. Before the suffering nature of the action is noticeable, it appears to be happiness; but when it is noticeable, it becomes the suffering of suffering. When

49

the suffering was not noticeable, the feeling was labeled "pleasure" and appeared as pleasure, but as you continue the action, the feeling gradually becomes suffering.

The peace you experience by abandoning desire leads you to nirvana, the sorrowless state. This peace, which is the absence of desire, allows you to develop completely, to become enlightened. You can experience this peace forever. From the very first time you free yourself from the thought of the worldly dharmas, from desire, you begin to develop this peace in your mental continuum, and eventually you experience it forever.

If you feel that by sacrificing desire you are sacrificing your happiness and are being left with nothing, remember that all your problems are based on desire and the thought of the worldly dharmas. Not knowing that the nature of desire is suffering, you cannot see that there is a better happiness. You cannot see that by sacrificing the thought of the worldly dharmas, by freeing your mind of desire, there is real peace, real happiness. This happiness doesn't depend on any external sense objects; it is developed within your own mind. With your mind you can develop this peace.

For example, let's say that you have a skin disease that makes you itch. You scratch yourself so much to relieve the itch that you make sores. Rather than labeling pleasure on the relief that scratching the itch gives you, wouldn't it be better not to have any disease at all? Wouldn't it be better to give up the disease? Having desire is like having this skin disease.

If there were no desire, there would be no cause for all the problems that arise from desire. There would be no evolution. If we didn't have this body, this samsara, caused by delusion and karma and contaminated by delusion's seed, we wouldn't have to experience hot and cold, hunger and thirst, and all the other problems. We wouldn't have to worry about our survival, or spend so much time and money looking after our body. We are kept busy just keeping this body looking good. From our hair down to our toes, we put so much work into decorating this body. So much of our precious human life is spent on that. When you get sick, however, even taking medicine cannot always cure you. So, wouldn't it be better not to have this body, this samsara, at all? Then you wouldn't have to experience all these problems.

Without desire, there would be much peace in the mind—a peace that could be developed and completed. This work has an end. Seeking samsaric pleasure in dependence upon external objects of desire is work that has no end. No matter how much you work towards that goal, it has no end. Like waves in the ocean coming one after the other, that work never ceases.

First of all, temporal happiness, which is dependent on external sense objects, is in the nature of suffering; and second, no matter what you do, there is no way to finish the work for temporal happiness.

LESS DESIRE, LESS PAIN

As Nagarjuna explains in the verse that Dromtönpa often recited:

Acquiring material things or not acquiring them; happiness or unhappiness; interesting or uninteresting sounds; praise or criticism: these eight worldly dharmas are not objects of my mind. They are all the same to me.

It is easy to understand how it can be a problem not to acquire things, to be unhappy, to hear uninteresting sounds, to have a bad reputation, to be criticized. These are commonly recognized as problems. But you might not recognize acquiring things, having comfort and happiness, hearing interesting sounds, having a good reputation and being praised as problems. However, they are all the same; they are all problems.

But the object itself is not the problem. Having wealth is not the problem. So, what is the problem? The problem is the mind desiring and clinging to wealth—*that* is the problem. Having a friend is not the problem; the mind clinging to the friend makes having a friend a problem.

Desire makes having these four—material things, comfort, interesting sounds, praise—a problem. If there's no desire, no worldly concern, having or not having these objects does not become a problem.

You might be sleeping comfortably one night when suddenly your sleep is disturbed by a mosquito biting you. If you have strong worldly concern, strong desire for comfort, you will be very annoyed at being bitten by the mosquito. Just being bitten, by just one mosquito. It is nothing dangerous, nothing that can cause any serious disease. The mosquito takes just a tiny, tiny drop of blood from your body. But seeing that mosquito's body filled with your own blood, you are shocked. You become angry at the mosquito and are upset all night. The next day, you complain about the mosquito all day long, "I couldn't sleep for hours last night!" Losing sleep for one night, or even a few hours, is like losing a precious jewel. You are as upset as somebody who has lost a million dollars. For some people, even such a small problem becomes huge.

There are also people who desire so much to be praised and respected by others. If you ignore such people and walk past them with your nose in the air, or say just one or two words disrespectfully, something that they don't expect to hear, it causes great pain in their minds. Or if you give them something in a disrespectful manner, whether purposely or not, again there is great pain. For such people with so much expectation, so much clinging, the pain from even a small physical action that they dislike is great. It feels like an arrow has been shot into their hearts.

Suddenly anger arises strongly. Suddenly their body becomes very tense. Their face, relaxed and peaceful before, now becomes kind of terrifying—swollen and tight, with their ears and nose turning red and the veins standing out on their forehead. Suddenly their whole character becomes very rough and unpleasant.

The greater people's desire to receive praise and respect, the greater the pain in their heart when they don't get it. It is similar with the other objects of desire. The stronger the desire for material things, comfort, interesting sounds, and praise, the greater the pain when they experience the opposite.

If you expect that a friend will always be pleasant, smiling, respectful, kind, and always do what you wish, but one day they unexpectedly do some small unpleasant thing, that tiny thing causes an incredible pain in your heart.

All this is related to worldly concern, to how strongly you desire something. The less desire you have for the four desirable objects, the fewer problems you will have when you meet the four undesirable objects. Less desire means less pain. If you cut off clinging to this life, there is no hurt when you experience criticism or do not receive something, because there is no clinging to praise or receiving things.

In the same way, when you do not cling to the expectation that your friend will always be nice to you, always smile at you, always help you when asked, there is no hurt when your friend changes and does the opposite to what you desire. There is no pain in your heart. Your mind is calm and peaceful. By cutting off the desire that clings to the four desirable objects, you don't have a problem when the four undesirable situations happen. They cannot hurt you, cannot disturb your mind.

The thought of the worldly dharmas clings to the four desirable objects of this life. Without this thought, there is so much calmness and peace in your mind that meeting the four undesirable objects doesn't bother you. And meeting the four desirable objects also doesn't bother you. If someone praises you, it doesn't matter; if someone criticizes you, it cannot disturb your mind. There is stability in your life, and peace of mind. There are no

53

ups and downs. This is equalizing the eight worldly dharmas.

How do you keep your mind peaceful when problems happen? How do you protect your mind so that experiencing the four undesirable things does not disturb you? By realizing that clinging to these four desirable objects is the problem. You have to realize the shortcomings of these four desirable objects and abandon clinging to them. This is the basic psychology. If you use this method, undesirable situations will not disturb you.

Geshe Chen-ngawa would equalize the eight worldly dharmas by reciting this verse:

> Being happy when life is comfortable and unhappy when it is uncomfortable: all activities for the happiness of this life should be abandoned like poison. Virtue and non-virtue are functions only of the mind. Cut off non-virtuous motivations and those motivations that are neither virtuous nor non-virtuous.

The latter refers to actions of body and speech with indeterminate motivations; these are called "unpredictable" actions.

The best way to train our mind is to expect the four undesirable objects rather than the four desirable ones. Expect to be criticized and disrespected. This practice of renunciation, which cuts off desire, is the best psychology. Having trained our mind to expect undesirable things, when something undesirable actually happens, it doesn't come as a shock to us; it doesn't hurt because we are expecting it.

Before knowing about Dharma, before practicing meditation, you regarded discomfort, uninteresting sounds, criticism, and not acquiring things as undesirable problems. Now, if you examine well the nature of the mind that clings to material things, comfort, interesting sounds, praise, you won't find that it is happy; you will see that it too is suffering. It is not the happiness you thought it was before knowing about Dharma. It is not peaceful—it is painful.

The mind that clings gets stuck to the object of desire. When you receive praise—"You are so intelligent," "You speak so well," "You understand Dharma so well"—your mind gets stuck to the praise and is no longer free. Like a body fastened with chains, the mind is fastened with attachment. The mind is tied, controlled, chained by attachment. The mind is stuck like glue to the object. Or like a moth flying into melted candle wax: its whole body, wings, and limbs become completely soaked in candle wax. Its body and limbs are so fragile that it is extremely difficult to separate them from the wax. Or like a fly that gets stuck in a spider's web: its limbs get completely wrapped in the web, and it is very difficult to separate them from it. Or like ants in honey. Attachment is the mind stuck to an object.

DESIRE IS THE SOURCE OF ALL PROBLEMS

As Lama Tsong Khapa mentions in *The Great Commentary on the Graduated Path to Enlightenment*:

> We follow desire in the hope of getting satisfaction,
> but following desire leads only to dissatisfaction.

In reality, the result of following desire is only dissatisfaction. You try again and again and again, but there is only dissatisfaction.

Following desire and not finding satisfaction is the major problem of samsara. Having cancer or AIDS, for example, is not the main problem. Compared to the problem of following desire and not finding satisfaction, cancer and AIDS are nothing; they don't continue from life to life. If you don't do something about the problem of desire in this life, while you have a perfect human rebirth, it will continue from life to life.

Following desire ties you to samsara continuously, so that again and again you experience the sufferings of the six realms. Again and again—endlessly. If you continuously follow desire, there is no real satisfaction, no real peace. Following desire leads you only to dissatisfaction and the continuous experience of the sufferings of samsara in one of the six realms.

It is the thought of the worldly dharmas that brings again and again all the diseases that scare us so much. Again and again, from life to life, it brings all the serious problems that a person can experience; it creates the karma for us to experience these problems again and again. The thought of the worldly dharmas, desire clinging to this life, is the most serious disease. Compared to the worldly dharmas, other problems are nothing.

If you do not have the thought of the worldly dharmas, which ties you to samsara, even if somebody kills you, all you do is change to another body. Your consciousness takes another perfect human body or goes to a pure realm. Your being killed is just a condition to change to another body. But if you have the thought of the worldly dharmas and do not practice Dharma, even though no one kills you and you live to be a hundred, you constantly use your perfect human rebirth to create the causes of the lower realms; you use your fortunate rebirth to create the causes of unfortunate rebirths with no opportunity to practice Dharma. The longer you live, the more negative karma you create, which causes you to abide in the lower realms and experience suffering for many eons. Therefore, this thought of the worldly dharmas is much more harmful than some enemy who merely kills you.

Lama Tsong Khapa's quotation about following desire continues:

> Desire brings so many other problems. Through following desire, the mind becomes rough and unpeaceful.

Hundreds of problems come from dissatisfaction. When there is very strong desire, it is very easy to become angry, for example. The stronger the clinging, the stronger the anger that arises. If you don't cling very much, you don't get so angry when someone upsets you.

You might still be disturbed, but less than before. Anger, jealousy, and so forth arise in relation to clinging. Because of clinging, these other negative thoughts arise. When any of these negative thoughts arises, you create negative karma, the cause of the lower realms.

When your mind is overwhelmed by desire, completely clouded by desire, you cannot meditate. Even if you have some idea of emptiness, for example, it is very difficult for you to have any feeling for it. At times when your mind is quiet and peaceful, you may have some feeling for it; but when your mind is clouded, a thick fog of desire covering everything, you are unable to meditate on emptiness. Furthermore, you are unable to think of the shortcomings of desire.

When you have strong desire for an object, you become very unhappy if you can't be near it. You cannot relax; there is no physical relaxation because there is no mental relaxation. Even though you may not have any particularly hard work to do, since your mind isn't relaxed because of desire, there is no physical comfort or relaxation.

There are many such examples of the shortcomings of desire. Think of alcoholics and drug addicts. Their lives become so unhappy, so uncontrolled, that they cannot do anything. Moreover, they damage their awareness and memory.

Disease comes from the dissatisfied mind of desire, the evil thought of the worldly dharmas, because dissatisfaction creates the conditions for sickness. You are then sick for many years, with huge unwanted expenses of many thousands of dollars. When you can't get money in a proper way, you have to steal. Your mind becomes disturbed; you have a nervous breakdown and go crazy. You then have to spend so much time and money on psychiatric consultations and might even end up in an institution.

And the origin of all this? One moment of uncontrolled desire. That one moment when you did not protect yourself from the thought of the worldly dharmas, when you did not practice

Dharma, brings so many problems. The problems go on and on for years and years, costing you a lot of money and making your life unnecessarily complicated and difficult. All these worries and expenses are caused by the thought of the eight worldly dharmas. If, from the very beginning, you had kept yourself free of the worldly dharmas, all those years of unwanted problems and expenses would not have happened. You need never have experienced them.

It is very clear that this is the source of AIDS, which comes when a person is controlled by the eight worldly dharmas. When I asked people with sexually transmitted AIDS what their mental state was when they started to experience symptoms, some said that it was one of very strong sexual desire. During the time of that non-virtuous mental state, they began to have fever, with sweating and weakness every day.

Basically all diseases, including AIDS and cancer, come from the thought of the worldly dharmas. Relationship problems, too: somehow if one does not attempt to have some control, relationship problems can go on and on and on. Life becomes hell—before going to actual hell, one experiences hell with a human body. There is hell in every direction. You feel completely trapped, suffocated. You cannot even breathe.

When your desire isn't fulfilled, when you can't get what you want, this is the time that nervous breakdowns and thoughts of committing suicide occur. Recently one Dharma student in Switzerland had problems like this and committed suicide. He hanged himself. I think he had heard some Dharma teachings but hadn't done much practice or retreat. He had a very good job earning a lot of money, but he had relationship problems.

You may have had the experience many times of thinking about suicide, about ending your human life, because of these kinds of problems. Basically, this is a shortcoming of the worldly thought of desire.

Kadampa Geshe Gönpawa, who had clairvoyance and many other realizations, said:

> If one receives the four desirable results of comfort, material things, interesting sounds, and praise from an action done with the thought of the eight worldly dharmas, that is the only result in this life, and there is no benefit in future lives. And if the four undesirable results come from the action, there is no benefit even in this life.

Often, actions done with the thought of the eight worldly dharmas that bring the four desirable results eventually lead to the four undesirable results anyway. For example, in business, you may have success after success; because of that success, you then act more and more with the thought of the worldly dharmas. After some time your karma for success finishes, and the karma of failure is experienced. In just one day you can become a beggar. One day, you are a millionaire; the next, you do not even know how you will pay your rent and take care of your family. Your whole life collapses.

This is due to doing actions with the thought of the worldly dharmas. Even though you have achieved material comfort, you are not satisfied and continue to act with the thought of the worldly dharmas. Because of your past success, one day your karma for success is exhausted, and everything collapses. Someone who was wealthy yesterday, with no financial worries, today suddenly has to worry even about such a basic thing as how to take care of his family. He doesn't know what to do and is unable to eat or sleep.

Even if you successfully steal one, two, three times, for example, your success cannot continue indefinitely. You need to have some control over your desire; you need to find some satisfaction. Otherwise, by continuing to steal, you will definitely get caught one day. No matter what the mistake is, by continuing to repeat it, one day it will definitely become a big problem. Another shortcoming of desire is that it eventually leads to so much that is undesirable.

Freeing yourself from desire is a great protection. Cutting off clinging to an object or person means that all the other negative minds do not arise, and you don't create all those negative karmas as a result. It provides unbelievable protection. Normally, by clinging to a particular object, you create much negative karma in relation to many other sentient beings. By cutting off clinging, you stop the causes of the lower realms.

Great peace comes when you free yourself from the thought of desire. Concentrate on this real peace that you can experience immediately by freeing yourself from desire. When you focus on this, there is no problem. When you attempt to attain this greater happiness, this real peace, temporal happiness becomes uninteresting and not too difficult to renounce—about as pleasant as picking up used toilet paper. If you are aware of this there is no danger of your becoming depressed or going crazy.

So we can see, no matter how many problems we have, there is no choice: we have to practice Dharma. And practicing Dharma means controlling our mind, controlling desire. Forget about living an ascetic life of pure Dharma practice; at the very least, for peace of mind and the happiness of this life, and to stop the increase of problems, we need to control desire.

ENDING SAMSARA

As Nagarjuna says:

> Actions generated from attachment, hatred, and ignorance are non-virtues. Actions generated from non-attachment, non-hatred, and non-ignorance are virtues. Whether virtuous or non-virtuous, actions are collected by the mind.

As long as we desire comfort, material things, respect, and a good reputation, and as long as we wish to avoid discomfort, not acquiring things, disrespect, and a bad reputation, every action is motivated by attachment, hatred, or ignorance. This means that there are far more non-virtuous actions than virtuous.

It says here in the text:

> It is extremely important to attempt not to generate desire for this life's happiness. If this desire arises, attempt to abandon it.

Also, Lama Atisha says:

> If the root is poisonous, the branches and leaves are also poisonous. If the root is medicinal, the branches and leaves are also medicinal. Like this, everything done with attachment, hatred, and ignorance is non-virtuous.

In other words, any activity—whether farming, business, fighting, helping friends and relatives, or meditating—done with the thought of the worldly dharmas, clinging to this life and motivated by attachment, anger, or ignorance becomes, as it says here, "only the cause of samsara and the lower realms."

The text continues:

> In order to take the essence, from the very beginning, one should not cling to this life.

"To take the essence" refers to this perfect human body.

Next comes a quotation from a tantric teaching, usually given as a motivation during preparation for a tantric initiation:

> Those with much devotion, who seek to go beyond samsara, are allowed to enter the mandala. One should not desire the results of this life.

This means that one should not seek happiness, comfort, material things, respect, reputation, and so forth, which are all of this life. The quotation continues:

> One who desires this life won't achieve the meaning that goes beyond samsara.

This means that the activities of those who desire this life won't become the cause of enlightenment, which is the state beyond samsara.

You can understand it in this way: If your aim is to achieve happiness only in this life, if that is your only expectation, everything you do—work, reciting prayers, taking initiations, eating, sleeping—does not become holy Dharma. All those actions are non-virtuous. Your hope is to get happiness, but the only thing you actually get from these actions is suffering. Even though you do your work with the aim of achieving happiness in this life, your actions actually become obstacles to this happiness and cause you to fail to find it. We can understand this if we look at both our own life experiences and those of others.

The quote concludes:

> Seeking to go beyond samsara will increase the happiness of this life's samsara.

This means that anyone who seeks only enlightenment, which is beyond samsara, and practices Dharma in order to achieve it, even though not seeking the happiness of this life, will find it naturally.

In *Letter to a Friend*, Nagarjuna says:

> If a spark lands on your hair or clothes and you're in danger of catching fire, you immediately brush it off.

In the same way, it is very worthwhile to attempt not to take rebirth.

When a spark falls on you, you get rid of it without delay. You react immediately even though the spark might only burn your hair or clothes. Surely you should be much more vigorous in trying to eliminate the causes of rebirth in the lower realms and the continuous sufferings of samsara.

All our problems arise because we have taken this samsaric rebirth, these aggregates caused by delusion and karma and contaminated by the seed of the delusions. Because we have taken rebirth, we experience pervasive, compounded suffering, and because of that, suffering of change and suffering of suffering. Not only do we experience these sufferings in this life, but this present samsara becomes the basis of all the future lives' samsaras and all the future lives' sufferings. Taking another samsara creates the cause of so many other future lives' samsaras. This process goes on and on.

Nagarjuna is saying that this situation is much more serious than having a small spark land on us, and that we should attempt not to take another rebirth. How can we attempt not to take rebirth? As mentioned in the teachings, craving is the chain that binds us to samsara; craving is the nearest cause of the future life's samsara. Not only does craving cause us to create negative karma right now during this life, but when we realize we are dying, we cling to our body, our aggregates. Craving and grasping at the time of death lead us to take the particular samsaric rebirth of our next life. Since craving is the major cause of samsara, cutting off craving becomes the essential Dharma practice in order not to take rebirth again. This is the way to end the continuum of samsara.

The conclusion is that all Dharma practitioners should renounce desire for the comfort of this life. Unless you renounce this, there is no way you can even be called "a Dharma practitioner." Everything done with desire seeking the comfort of this life is not Dharma. As long as there's desire, there is no practice of Dharma. There is a Tibetan saying: Since a horse doesn't have the character of a lion, don't call a horse a lion.

One Kadampa geshe, Lama Gyampa, says:

> Renouncing this life is the very start of Dharma. You don't do a single Dharma practice but feel proud of being a Dharma practitioner—how foolish! Check whether your mental continuum contains the very first step of Dharma: renouncing this life.

Even if you think that you are not a religious person, since you don't want problems and do want happiness, you still must control desire. There is no other solution. You cannot reduce desire and the other delusions by taking medicine, having an operation, or by other external means. The method is to think of the shortcomings of desire, and that life is short. This is the essential psychology, even if you are not a Buddhist and don't want to be a Buddhist. There is no other solution. In order to have fewer problems in your life, you must reflect on the shortcomings of desire. If desire is eliminated, problems no longer exist. As soon as you abandon desire, you won't see any more problems.

Practicing bodhicitta helps to control desire. Exchanging oneself for others, which means renouncing oneself and cherishing others (see chapter 9), or having a very good heart, wanting to eliminate the sufferings of others and obtain their happiness, solves many problems.

One whose mind is not strong enough to practice bodhicitta should stop problems of desire by reflecting on meditations such as the perfect human rebirth and, especially, impermanence and death (see chapter 7). You can stop desire by remembering that life is very short and that death can happen at any moment, and relating these thoughts to the lower realms, karma, and so forth.

As I mentioned before, Shantideva's "secret of the mind" is not some high realization. Realizing the shortcomings of the eight worldly dharmas and reflecting on impermanence and death can also be seen as secrets of the mind.

Meditating on impermanence and death and recognizing the shortcomings of desire—which means seeing that all problems arise from it—give you the strength to make the determination to renounce this life, to cut clinging to this life. These two strengthen you and weaken the worldly dharmas. They give you the strength to cut off clinging to this life, to free yourself from desire.

If you do not realize these secrets of the mind, even though you want happiness and don't want suffering, you experience the opposite. Devoid of temporal and ultimate happiness, you wander in samsara, continuously experiencing suffering. But if you do realize these secrets of the mind, the supreme meaning of the Dharma, you are able to achieve happiness and eliminate suffering and will not wander aimlessly in samsara.

6

Subduing the Mind

If you neglect to protect your mind,
you can neither close the door to suffering
nor open the door to happiness.

Do not commit any non-virtuous actions,
Practice perfect virtue,
Subdue your own mind:
This is the teaching of the Buddha.

𝒲HEN WE RECITE TOGETHER this verse of the Buddha, we should remember, as Kirti Tsenshab Rinpoche has explained, that it contains the four noble truths. You are experiencing true suffering (the first noble truth), which is undesirable, and you need to achieve ultimate happiness, the cessation of all suffering (third), which depends upon ceasing the entire true cause of suffering (second); and achieving this depends upon actualizing the entire true path (fourth).

The very essence of this verse is not to commit any non-virtuous actions. Thinking that the source of life's suffering and problems is external is itself the problem. Separating our own mind from the origin of problems and blaming external sources, such as other people or objects, only brings more problems. Thinking in this way—and also thinking that happiness comes from out-side—we do nothing with our own mind. This mind that has been unsubdued for beginningless rebirths is left alone, still unsubdued. Nothing is developed, nothing is changed. Constantly we create the cause of suffering in future lives, and create problems even now in this life.

It is good to relate this verse to our past problems, and it is especially effective to relate *subdue your own mind* to our pride, anger, jealousy, desire, and thick ignorance. Subduing these delusions is the teaching of the Buddha. Not subduing them is not the teaching of the Buddha—in other words, not doing anything about our delusions but keeping busy doing many other so-called spiritual practices is not the teaching of the Buddha.

Delusions make the mind unhappy, unpeaceful, unsubdued. Even though our actions may look like Dharma and be called "Dharma" or "spiritual practice," they are not the teaching of the Buddha unless they destroy delusions. One definition of Dharma is *any remedy for the delusions.* If an action that is done in the name of Christianity or some other religion is a remedy for the delusions—subduing anger, attachment, ignorance, and selfishness—it is Dharma. Anything that is not a remedy for delusion is not Dharma.

As His Holiness the Dalai Lama says, Dharma is anything that mends or fixes the mind. When some object is broken, mending it is good because it allows you to gain happiness or the means of living for yourself and for others. Like this, Dharma mends the mind. Without harming the delusions, no method can fix the mind. There is no way to improve the mind without decreasing the delusions. Delusions have to be eliminated.

In order to bring happiness to yourself and others, Dharma has to be the remedy for the delusions. If Dharma helps the delusions, then no matter how much we practice, we will not see any improvement in the mind; in fact, it will become worse and worse: more and more unsubdued, harder and harder. Even though you may always be hearing Dharma, speaking Dharma, reading Dharma, or living in a Dharma center, even though your whole life revolves around Dharma, if your delusions increase, then your spiritual practice is helping your delusions instead of harming them. If your pride, anger, desire, and so forth increase, your Dharma education is creating negative karma instead of purifying what you have already created.

In order for you to receive happiness from Dharma, your practice has to harm the delusions. For example, a medicine that only causes more infection and pain is not harming the disease but hindering the cure. Medicine is supposed to cure sickness, not make it worse.

Subdue your own mind is only one line, but it covers all the obscurations, from seeing mistakes in the guru up to the subtle dual views of the three visions: the appearances of the white path, increasing red path, and near-attainment dark path, and even to the last, most subtle obscuration that prevents the achievement of omniscient mind. *Subdue your own mind* covers all these wrong conceptions.

This is the teaching of the Buddha because to subdue your own mind is the source of happiness. Subduing your own mind is the main teaching of the Buddha. Every single word that Buddha taught is for subduing one's own mind; there is no other purpose. Every single word of all the 84,000 teachings—the Hinayana, Paramitayana, secret Vajrayana teachings—is for subduing the mind.

Remember the kindness of the compassionate founder, Guru Shakyamuni Buddha, in revealing all these teachings of both the causal and resultant paths. Buddha revealed the complete path to enlightenment through all these different levels of teachings, in accordance with the capacities of sentient beings' minds. Right now we have the freedom and opportunity to listen to and reflect and meditate upon this unmistaken path; we can create the unmistaken cause for any happiness that we wish. All this is due to the kindness of Shakyamuni Buddha in giving his teachings.

Shakyamuni Buddha revealed the path that guides us to happiness; he revealed the path that gives us the freedom to understand and to create the causes to have happiness in future lives, liberation, and enlightenment. He helps us to develop our potential, our Buddha-nature. By meeting the teachings and practicing them, we can develop our Buddha-nature and thus achieve enlightenment.

By meditating on the path revealed by Buddha, we can gradually develop our Buddha-nature and thus fulfill the wishes of all sentient beings. It is due to the kindness of Shakyamuni Buddha that we can achieve omniscient mind, perfect power, and perfect compassion for all sentient beings.

Everything, including happiness and suffering, is dependent upon the mind. If you do not subdue your mind, suffering arises; your own mind produces this suffering. By subduing your mind, you experience happiness. This is why the happiness of sentient .beings depends on the existence of Buddha's teachings.

Since everything is dependent on our own mind, we have to subdue our own mind. We have to give up wrong thoughts, which are the cause of suffering and which bring problems to ourselves and to numberless others, now and in life after life. If these wrong thoughts are eliminated, there is only happiness; there is no cause of problems, no creator of problems. The more we eliminate these false conceptions, the more and more happiness there is.

PROTECTING YOUR MIND

In *A Guide to the Bodhisattva's Way of Life*, Shantideva explains:

> All the tigers, lions, elephants, snakes, enemies, guardians of the hells, black magicians, and cannibals are tied up by tying up this one mind.

Tying the mind away from negative thoughts, not allowing it to run after anger, desire, ignorance, and so forth, means that you stop creating negative karma. When you prevent your mind from being controlled by delusions, you don't create negative karma, so you don't experience the result of other beings harming you and endangering your life.

For example, Devadatta always tried to compete with and harm Guru Shakyamuni Buddha. One day when Buddha was begging for alms, Devadatta sent a crazy elephant to attack him. However, instead of harming Buddha, the elephant became completely subdued when it came into his presence. I also heard that mosquitoes never bit His Holiness Song Rinpoche. And there is a similar story about the Italian saint, St. Francis of Assisi, who lived at the same time as Milarepa, the great Tibetan yogi who achieved enlightenment in one brief lifetime.

In a forest there lived a wolf that had harmed many people. When St. Francis was told about it, he said, "I will go and talk to the wolf." Some people told St. Francis not to go because the wolf might attack him, but St. Francis insisted.

So, St. Francis went into the forest to talk to the wolf. When the wolf came close to St. Francis, instead of harming him, it became completely subdued. Like a dog with its master, the wolf became very tame, lying down and licking St. Francis's feet. St. Francis told the wolf that he would give it food, and that it shouldn't harm anybody any more. From that time, the wolf stopped attacking people.

St. Francis's body is kept at Assisi, which is near Istituto Lama Tzong Khapa. Lama Yeshe and I visited Assisi. Lama did a short meditation in the tomb where St. Francis's holy body is kept. There is also a waterfall near Assisi, and it is said that if the water dries up, it will be very inauspicious for Italy. St. Francis also had a disciple-nun who herself had three hundred disciples.

During St. Francis's life, one of the caves had water dripping from its roof. Some of his disciples complained that they could not meditate because of the noise of the water. St. Francis, who called most things "sister" or "brother," went to the cave and said to the water, "Sister, please stop, otherwise my disciples cannot meditate." The water then stopped.

Such stories are common in the life stories of bodhisattvas. There are many stories of great Tibetan and Indian yogis who had rivers stop flowing to allow them to cross and then start flowing again once they were safely across. In Tibet, when a huge flood was coming towards the monastery of the bodhisattva

Jampa Monlam, he wrote on a rock, "If it is true that I have bodhicitta, the flood will turn back." Jampa Monlam placed the rock in the path of the flood, which then subsided. These stories prove the power of bodhicitta, the ultimate good heart.

By tying the mind to virtue, protecting it from delusions, you don't create negative karma, so there are no dangers to your life. Also, because of bodhicitta, your mind is subdued. Tying your mind to virtue and away from disturbing thoughts is like tying up all dangerous beings: tigers, snakes, hell guardians, enemies. If you have bodhicitta, even the elements cannot harm you; due to the power of bodhicitta, you are able to control the elements. By tying this one mind to bodhicitta, you tie up all those numberless dangerous animals and enemies. Taming this one thing, your mind, also tames all those others.

If you wanted to tie up all the dangerous animals on this earth, your life wouldn't be long enough. And even if you aren't reborn in this particular world but on another planet, as long as you have karma and delusions, you will meet enemies and dangerous animals. As long as the mind is unsubdued, there is always outside harm. Once the mind is subdued, once there is no anger in the mental continuum, there is no outside enemy. When it is impossible for anger to arise within you, you find no outside enemies anywhere. An outside enemy exists only if there is anger inside.

Without delusion, there is no negative karma, so no one harms you. In addition to this, when your mind is patient in nature, even if someone criticizes, beats, or kills you, you recognize no outside enemy. When you have completed the perfection of patience, you see the other person as your best friend, even while they are criticizing, beating, or killing you. As long as your mind is in the nature of patience during that time, you don't see any outside enemy harming you, only someone benefiting you. But as soon as your mind changes to anger, you see that person as harming you.

Opening the Door of Dharma says here:

> What is the use of any conduct apart from the conduct of protecting the mind?

This is very good to remember in your day-to-day life. If you forget to protect your own mind, what is the use of any traditional form of discipline? If the mind is not protected, you cannot stop your suffering and problems.

Even though you may do hundreds of other things, if you leave out this most important practice, you cannot stop your problems and achieve happiness, especially ultimate happiness. This is very good to remember. People who recite many, many prayers and millions of mantras all day long are wasting their time if they forget to protect their mind. Your mind is the source of all your own suffering and happiness. If you neglect to protect your mind, you can neither close the door to suffering nor open the door to happiness.

In the West, there are so many rules: you can't do this, you can't do that. Sometimes I think there are too many rules. Once I was staying in Sydney in a house that had a swimming pool and a spa. A few people were playing in the pool and jumping from the diving board. The next door neighbors got very upset. They complained that there was too much noise and called the police.

I was in my room. I didn't look outside, but I heard the police arrive. By the way the car was driven, they seemed annoyed. The neighbors told the police that the people in our pool were disturbing them. The police thought they were talking nonsense and simply left, even though they had come all the way from the city. That same afternoon the neighbors' children made a lot of noise.

No matter how many rules are made, as long as protecting the mind is not emphasized in school or university or in the culture, problems go on and on and on. Everyone has to protect their own mind. Instead of "An apple a day keeps the doctor away," we could say "Protecting the mind every day keeps the police away"!

7

Remembering Impermanence and Death

If one does not remember death, one does not remember Dharma.

$\mathcal{M}$EDITATE: LOOK AT EVERYTHING—self, action, object; friend, enemy, stranger, who are the objects of your attachment, anger, and ignorance; all causative phenomena—with awareness of the reality: all these are transitory, and can cease at any time. Not only do all these phenomena change within each second due to causes and conditions, but they can cease at any time.

Death can happen at any moment, even to you. Death can happen at any moment to the friend, enemy, or stranger. Your possessions also deteriorate, and not only do they change within each second, but they can also be separated from you at any time.

Therefore, there is no reason at all to allow discriminating thoughts of attachment, anger, or ignorance to arise in relation to these objects. Be aware that these things are transitory in nature and not permanent.

The main remedy to the thought of the worldly dharmas is meditation on impermanence and death. If one does not remember death, one does not remember Dharma. And even if one remembers Dharma, if one does not remember impermanence and death, one does not practice Dharma.

Even though you may accept that you can die at any time, in your daily life you tend to think that you are not going to die soon—not this year, not this week, not today, not now. Because of this, you postpone your practice of Dharma. Even if you practice Dharma, if you don't think about impermanence and death, it does not become pure Dharma.

If you don't think about impermanence and death, you don't practice Dharma, which means protecting karma by abandoning non-virtue and practicing virtue; and you constantly create negative karma instead. Then at the time of death you become very upset and fearful, which means you are already experiencing the signs of going to the lower realms. Many terrifying appearances can come to you at the time of death.

If you remember impermanence and death, you lead a highly meaningful life. You are able to practice the paths of three levels of capability and achieve the three great purposes: the happiness of future lives, liberation, and enlightenment. Remembering impermanence and death is also a very easy way to control delusions. You can overpower your delusions.

Remembering impermanence and death is very meaningful. It is very important at the beginning of Dharma practice, as it helps you to actually begin your practice, and then again to continue it so that you succeed in your attempt to achieve enlightenment. Then when death happens, you can die happily. The great yogi Milarepa, who achieved enlightenment in one brief lifetime of this degenerate age, expressed his personal experience of this:

> Being scared of death, I escaped to the mountains.
> Now, having realized the ultimate nature of the primordial mind, even if death comes, I am not worried.

CLOSER AND CLOSER TO DEATH

Death is definite. No medicine can stop death, and there is no place where we don't experience death. No matter how powerful our body is, our life shortens without any break. Each time we recite the mantra *om mani padme hung* and move a bead on our mala, our life is closer to death with each mantra we finish. When we leave here to go home, each step we take brings us closer to death. When we arrive home, that much of our life is finished. When we drink a cup of tea, with each sip we take, our life is closer to death. When we finish the cup of tea, that much of our life has gone; we are that much nearer to death. Each time we breathe in and out, our life is nearer and nearer to death.

Meditate while looking at a clock or watch: as each second passes, in reality our life is closer to death—but not because we're wearing a watch! Looking at a watch is a very powerful way to meditate on impermanence and death. With each second you are coming closer to death.

When we eat a plate of rice, each time the spoon goes to our mouth, our life is finishing. When we finish that plate of rice, that much of our life has gone, and we are that much closer to the time of our death. When we read a newspaper, as we finish each page, we are that much nearer to death. When we talk to people, as we finish each word, we are closer to death. When we complete each sentence, that much of our life has already gone. When we gossip for hours, that much of our life is finished; when we stand up and walk away, our life is that much closer to death.

And once part of our life is over, we can't bring it back or change it. When a boxer or racing-car driver injures his body, it can usually be fixed, and this can happen many times. But once our life has passed, whether it has been meaningful or wasted, it has gone forever. You can't fix up any part of your life that has passed; all you can do is work on the present and future. By making your present life more meaningful, you can fix up the future; you can make a better future.

The lam-rim mentions that a life of one hundred years can be divided into two parts: one half is spent sleeping—this is without counting daytime sleeping!—and much of the other fifty years of waking time passes in quarreling, sickness, and many other meaningless activities. If we add up all the time spent on what we call practicing Dharma, it is very little.

And then you have to die. Even though you have a perfect human body, even though you haven't found time to practice Dharma during your lifetime, you still have to die.

THE TIME OF DEATH IS UNCERTAIN

Right now there are people dying in hospital: people with AIDS or cancer whose cases the doctors regard as hopeless, with only one day, a few hours, a few minutes to live. They are regarded as dying because they are close to death, but they still have a short time left to live. They are not dead yet. Think, "It is the same with me—I am also dying." It is not that if you have AIDS or cancer, you die, and if you don't have AIDS or cancer, you don't die or don't die soon. It is not like that. Meditate this way when you get up in the morning. Remember that you are dying also, just like the people in hospital who are regarded as dying. Using the same reasoning, you do not have much time left to live.

You may even die before those people with cancer who are regarded as dying. You may reason that because they have a certain disease, they will die soon. But this doesn't necessarily follow; it is not logical. Many healthy people who did not have AIDS or cancer have died today. The question of death does not depend on having disease; even dying soon does not depend on having disease. Even for the healthy, it is the same: death can happen at any time.

You are dying. Second by second you are getting nearer to death—there is not much time left. Life is very short. The people with serious diseases are regarded as dying; those who come to visit them are regarded not as dying but as living. But in reality there is no difference. Both are the same in getting constantly nearer to death, and in not having much time left.

On top of all this, death can happen to you at any moment. The actual time of death isn't definite, and there are three reasons for this. First, generally in the world nothing is definite, and during degenerate times such as these, life is even more indefinite. Second, there are few conditions for living and many conditions for death, and even the conditions we need for survival can become causes of death.

Life is full of conditions for death. All the delusions within our minds—such as the thought of the worldly dharmas, which induces other negative minds that bring heavy obstacles and heavy karma—are conditions for death. Until now you may not have had any obstacles to your life. Suddenly, today, because of not practicing Dharma and not controlling your mind, you may create heavy negative karma by breaking vows or in relation to sentient beings or holy objects. Suddenly there may be life obstacles, with signs of death in your dreams or other things happening. Even though you do have the karma to live, suddenly there is danger of death. There are many conditions for death inside your own mind, and in external conditions, which are also created by your mind.

Third, this body is very fragile, like a water bubble. Negative ways of thinking disturb the winds within your body, which then disturb the four elements. Disturbance of the elements causes disease and brings the danger of death. As explained in a commentary on Kalachakra, the inner and outer elements are related. If the four inner elements are disturbed, the outside elements are also disturbed. These can then threaten your health and your life, even becoming the conditions for your death.

SO MANY PEOPLE HAVE DIED ALREADY

Many people we have known, who have been close to us, have died. Remember His Holiness Ling Rinpoche and His Holiness Serkong Rinpoche, gurus of His Holiness the Dalai Lama? They have already left their holy bodies. Those of you who have met and heard teachings from them will remember them; His Holiness Ling Rinpoche gave Yamantaka initiation during the first Dharma Celebration.

Our kind Lama Yeshe, kinder than all the three times' Buddhas, has also gone. During the time we spent with him, he was very real to us, laughing and making jokes. We enjoyed so much being with him and receiving teachings from him; he seemed somehow permanent, truly existent, real. But all that has gone now; we have just the memories. That aspect doesn't exist any more.

Lama Yeshe's brother, Geshe Thinley, was always joking and looked permanent. He has also died; he doesn't exist now. Those of you who are familiar with Kopan will remember the Nepali caretaker who came to milk the buffaloes every morning. He lived there a long time, and actually helped us to buy the land on which Kopan Monastery is built. When we saw him every day, he looked kind of permanent. Now he too is gone. So many people you knew have already died.

Even someone as famous as Mao Zedong has died. Even though he had a large army and frightened many people, he doesn't exist now. Indira Gandhi was also well known to the world, with her pictures everywhere. Despite her popularity and military power, she is gone; she doesn't exist now.

By this time next year it is possible that, like those who have already died, only your name will be left. Of those who have died, there are now left only their names written in letters, their pictures, and people still mentioning them. By this time next year, this could have happened to you. Nothing to be seen—only your name to talk about and pictures to look at.

As you do in tantric practice, bring into the present what is going to happen in the future. Meditate on your death now. Think of your body in a coffin being taken from your home to the cemetery, being buried there under the ground. Or meditate on your body in a coffin about to be cremated. Only your possessions are left. Think about this.

When death happens, even though the body completely disintegrates, the consciousness continues. When the butter in a butter lamp finishes, the flame stops, but the consciousness is not like that. The consciousness continues from life to life.

At the moment you cannot remember past lives or see future

84

lives, but you cannot use that as a reason to say that there are no past and future lives. To be able to say that and contradict those people who can see their own and others' past and future lives, you must have omniscient mind or at least the clairvoyance that brings that ability. Only then can you judge. But there is no omniscient or clairvoyant mind that sees that there are no past lives.

The inability to see past lives is ignorance, not clairvoyance. Only if you have clairvoyance can you judge whether past and future lives exist. Since you cannot argue that you have all the realizations and knowledge that others have, you cannot say that other people's memories of past and future lives are wrong. The simple fact is that even if you don't remember past and future lives, there are others with clearer minds, which means thinner obscurations, and more realizations who *can* see past and future lives.

Think about karma and rebirth. The answer to whether you will have a good or bad rebirth depends on whether your karma is good or bad. Remember that your death can happen suddenly. You may be active, working, when suddenly your eyes roll up and you die. You may even experience the signs of going to the lower realms. Suddenly, in the middle of doing something, your body becomes a corpse, with no breathing, no movement. This can happen to you at any time.

TOMORROW MAY BE TOO LATE

Recently, I came across this newspaper article:

> *Johannesburg* (AFP): A South African businessman collapsed and died moments after making a speech warning that death could come at any time, a Sunday newspaper reported here. Danny Dudoit, 49, is believed to have choked to death on a peppermint minutes after delivering a speech on the need to live for the moment at the toast-masters' club meeting near

here last week. The last words Dudoit spoke were, "You must enjoy life while you can, tomorrow may be too late."

He sat down to a big ovation and when the next speaker began talking the audience heard him making choking sounds. "At first we thought he was having an epileptic fit," said the president of the toast-masters' club, Joh Vanseck, "then we realized he had stopped breathing and a guest from another club pumped his chest and gave him the kiss of life." Then Vanseck said that paramedics called to the scene had also tried to save Dudoit but something was blocking his windpipe. There was no food around, the only thing he could have eaten was a peppermint. "We were all very shocked," said Vanseck, "that his speech proved to be so prophetic. It was uncanny."

When the speaker said that you must enjoy life, he didn't clarify how to enjoy life, so there is still a problem. He missed the point that one needs to practice Dharma.

There is another story of someone who came back from the East, where he had made many movies. While he was showing one of his movies to a group of people, they saw something strange reflected on the screen. When they turned around to look, they found him dead in his chair. People have also died while drinking tea; just before the cup reaches their lips, they die in their chair. People die before finishing the food on their plate. Every day people are dying in the middle of doing something. This happens every day.

WHAT ARE YOU GOING TO DO WITH YOUR LIFE?

So, we need to do something to make this life meaningful. This is the same for people who have AIDS or cancer, who may have a short life, and for perfectly healthy people.

The best thing to do is to recite every morning, "I am going to die today." This cuts off all problems. Once you make this decision, there are no more problems. Problems come from your wrong ideas, your wrong conceptions. Thinking that you are going to die today cuts off these conceptions and problems.

After you have made this decision, it is very good to remember this verse from *Lama Chöpa*:

> Cherishing myself is the source of all sufferings, while cherishing others is the basis of all qualities. Please grant me blessings to do the heart practice, the yoga of exchanging myself for others.

You are going to die today—so what are you going to do with your life? Just thinking that you are going to die today is not sufficient; the thought should persuade you to practice Dharma and not waste your life. What are you going to do? Whether you live another hour or another hundred years, what are you going to do with your life?

Suddenly you have the answer: the heart practice is contained in the above verse. Whether or not you are able to recite many prayers, study extensively, or sit in meditation, this is the essential, most meaningful practice. Simply by thinking of the words of this verse—that cherishing the self is the basis of all obstacles and sufferings, and cherishing others the basis of all qualities—you are able to change the object of your concern. Before, your concern was only for yourself, but just by saying these words, you change the object of your concern from the self to the other sentient beings suffering in the six realms.

Constantly keep the thought of other sentient beings in place of the I. Change from cherishing the I to cherishing others. Always hold this thought in your heart and do all your actions on the basis of this attitude. From morning to night, do everything—meditation, prayers, study, eating, talking—on the basis of this attitude. In your heart, do everything for all sentient beings.

8

Finding No Self to Cherish

Since the I that exists is merely imputed,
there is nothing to cherish, nothing to cling to.

LIVING IN A HALLUCINATION

OUR WHOLE PROBLEM IS not being aware of the reality of things. Just like hallucinogenic drugs or mushrooms, wrong conceptions make our minds hallucinate. We are unable to practice awareness of reality—that is, that all causative phenomena are transitory and, the basic thing, that what appears to us does not exist in the way that it appears to exist.

The ignorance in our mind that holds everything as truly existent focuses on the I that does exist, but apprehends a truly existent I, which doesn't exist. Like this, everything our ignorance focuses on—I, body, mind, others, six sense objects—does exist, but not in the way ignorance apprehends it. That is the hallucination.

Look at all your projections of true existence. Just as this brocade cloth covers the table, the truly existent I covers the mere I. In your own view the subject, the I, is covered with true existence, as are the action and the object. They are all decorated with the appearance of true existence. Look at all these things, aware that they are empty. Concentrate on the fact that everything—subject, action, object—is empty. Every single thing that exists is completely empty.

Concentrate on emptiness. In emptiness, there is no I and other, no subject and object, no friend and enemy. In emptiness, there is no attachment, no anger. In emptiness, there is no emptiness. While meditating on emptiness, while you are looking at emptiness, think this. Then it makes sense. There is not the slightest reason to believe that anything exists from its own side.

The I, which is merely imputed, which is labeled on the aggregates, does not exist in the way it is seen by our ignorance. Ignorance holds the I not as merely labeled but as existing from its own side. This truly existent aspect held by ignorance does not exist. We have to be aware that what appears to exist from its own side is empty of existing from its own side.

All things that exist, starting with the I, are nothing other than what is merely imputed. There is no I other than what is merely imputed. There are no aggregates, no body, no mind, other than what is merely imputed. Similarly, action, object, friend, enemy, stranger, possessions, sense objects, all these are nothing other than what is merely imputed by the mind. All of these are completely empty, almost as if they don't exist.

But all these—self, action, object, friend, enemy, stranger, possessions, happiness, unhappiness, good reputation, bad reputation, praise, criticism, acquiring things, not acquiring things—are *not* non-existent. It is as if they are illusory, as if they do not exist; but they are not illusory—they do exist.

Look at all these things as illusory. What appears to you—real self, real action, real object, real friend, real enemy, real stranger, real possessions—has nothing to do with reality. This real existence from its own side has nothing to do with reality. In reality, all these are completely empty.

Happiness, unhappiness, praise, criticism, pleasant sounds, unpleasant sounds, good reputation, bad reputation, getting things, not getting things—the appearance of all these as real, existing from their own side, has nothing to do with reality. Not even an atom of them exists in this way. In reality, all these are completely empty.

Due to imprints left on our mental continuum by our past ignorance, which held everything to be truly existent, again we project true existence onto all these things now, which in reality are merely imputed. The seed, or potential, left on the mental continuum is actualized in this way.

Nothing exists without labeling. The I doesn't exist without labeling "I." The aggregates, samsara, nirvana—nothing exists without labeling. Therefore, everything is empty. Everything that appears to exist from its own side—self, action, object, friend, enemy, stranger, sense objects—is completely empty.

From morning to night, we talk about things that are merely imputed, think things that are merely imputed, hear things that are merely imputed, look at things that are merely imputed. From morning to night, from birth to death, from beginningless rebirth to enlightenment, everything is like this.

So there is no reason at all to generate attachment, anger, and ignorance. It is complete nonsense, unnecessary and meaningless. Without reason, your mind has created these problems. Your own mind has made up ignorance, attachment, and anger. The conclusion is that there is no reason at all for discriminating thoughts of attachment, anger, and ignorance to arise.

Looking for the I

None of the aggregates is the I. Even the whole group of the aggregates is not the I. The body is not the I. Even the mind is not the I. Understand clearly that none of these is the I. The aggregates are the base upon which we label "I," but they are not the I; the I is something other than that. The I is not separate from the aggregates, but it is different from the aggregates.

From the top of your head down to your toes, the I is nowhere to be found. All this that you can point to is not the I. All this that you can touch is not the I. Nothing of this is the I. Be clear about this: the I is nowhere. Meditate on this.

If the I could be found on the aggregates, it would mean that it exists from its own side, that the I is truly existent. By using scientific analysis, not just by relying on faith, you cannot find the I on these aggregates. But this does not mean that the I doesn't exist. There is no I on these aggregates—but there is an I. There is an I in this world, in this Root Institute in Bodhgaya.

The I exists—why? Because the I is experiencing suffering and can abandon suffering by abandoning its causes. Because of the suffering, the I is practicing Dharma.

If there were no I, life would be very simple—you could just relax. You wouldn't have to worry about getting up in the morning and rushing off to work. You wouldn't need to look for a job. If there were no I, why would you need to work? Or go to university to get a degree? All this would not be necessary. There would be no I to experience happiness and comfort, so why would you bother to do any of these things? If there were no I, why would you worry? You could stop all these activities immediately.

If there were no I, there would be no action of meditating. If there were no subject, how could there be an action of meditating? It would be lying to say, "I am meditating." There wouldn't be subject, action, or object.

However, since there is a base, since the base of the I exists, there is no choice: the I exists. Since there is an action that results in suffering, there is no choice: non-virtue exists. Since there are secondary thoughts that disturb the principal consciousness, there is no choice: delusion exists. Since there are undesirable, uncomfortable, unpeaceful feelings, there is no choice: suffering exists.

LOOKING FOR LAMA ZOPA

When you look at me, there seems to be a real Lama Zopa existing from the side of the object, but this is completely opposite to reality. The way that Lama Zopa appears to exist is not the way that Lama Zopa really exists.

We are living our lives in a big hallucination. We lack the awareness that the way everything appears to us as real from its own side is a hallucination. The "real" Lama Zopa means the one that has existence from its own side. When we say "real" we actually mean "truly existent." If you do not see things as illusory, when you talk of "real," you mean "truly existent."

There is no Lama Zopa on these aggregates. That real Lama Zopa from its own side cannot be found. From the top of my head down to my toes, there is no Lama Zopa here. Lama Zopa is nowhere to be found: in this world, in Bodhgaya, in these aggregates. It is nowhere.

The whole group of the five aggregates—form, feeling, recognition, compounded aggregates, consciousness—is not Lama Zopa, and none of the aggregates individually is Lama Zopa. To express it another way: besides this body not being Lama Zopa, even this mind is not Lama Zopa. Lama Zopa cannot be found anywhere from the crown of my head down to my toes. This is a simple, short, and effective way to meditate on emptiness.

But Lama Zopa is *not* non-existent. At this time what is called "Lama Zopa" exists in this world, in India, in Bodhgaya, in Root Institute. Right now, in Root Institute, Lama Zopa is performing the function of talking, with noises coming from the mouth (and the nose, from time to time!). But the existence of Lama Zopa is something completely other than what you normally think. The reality is something else, completely something else.

The reality of the way Lama Zopa exists is extremely subtle, something that we don't normally think about. The way we normally apprehend Lama Zopa has nothing to do with the way Lama Zopa exists. The way Lama Zopa exists is completely something else.

So, how does Lama Zopa exist? What is the I? If you label "I" on a table, a bicycle, a car, a rock, how do you feel? If you label on a TV set what you usually label on the aggregates, how do you feel?

Let's say there is a scarecrow in a field, protecting the crops from the crows. When you are at a distance and unable to see it clearly, you may think it is a person. When you get nearer, you see that it is only a scarecrow. How do you feel when what you have previously labeled as a person turns out to be a scarecrow? How do you feel about your previously imputed label of person?

How do you feel when a relative dies and you are left with just their empty name? How do you feel about that name? The person is dead; you cannot see their body; there is nothing you can see—so, how do you feel about their name? They seem like illusions, don't they?

This is how those who have realized emptiness feel about actual living beings. They understand everything in this way: the I, all existence, samsara and nirvana. Those experienced meditators see everything as illusory—and this is reality. This is how everything exists in reality.

The way things exist is extremely subtle, almost as if they don't exist. You cannot say that they completely don't exist, but it is very easy to say that they don't exist, to come to the point of nihilism. It is a very subtle point. You can see why so many people have difficulty understanding the *Prasangika-Madhyamika* view of subtle dependent arising.

We become so confused. Our problem is that if we accept that something exists, we tend to think it exists from its own side. It is difficult to understand that something can still exist while being empty of existing from its own side—that is, not truly existent in nature. It is hard to accept these two views on the basis of one object.

Because these two views are difficult to unify, many people fall into the extreme view of saying that the object does not exist. They are unable to enter the Middle Way. They assert that if an object does not exist from its own side, there is no way that it can exist. Such people then arrive at the philosophy that nothing exists, and that what appears to exist is a hallucination.

The correct view is extremely subtle. By analyzing the example of Lama Zopa, you can see that it is extremely subtle. Lama Zopa exists in dependence upon the aggregates. It is as simple as that. This is the reason that Lama Zopa is here, now, in this tent. Lama Zopa exists in dependence upon the aggregates; that is why he is here. But what Lama Zopa is is extremely subtle, which is why I say it is *as if* it doesn't exist, *as if* it is an illusion.

LOOKING FOR THINGS OTHER THAN THE I

In a similar way that you meditate on the selflessness of persons relating to your own I, you can meditate on the selflessness of the aggregates, or of everything else that exists. Those not familiar with the subject may not realize that this *self* in selflessness can refer to anything; it does not necessarily refer to the person, or self. There is also the selflessness of the aggregates.

Look at everything here: table, brocade, light, walls, curtains, flowers, action, object, sense objects. You have to understand that the way all these things are appearing to us is a complete hallucination. By analyzing the example of Lama Zopa, you can see how we are completely trapped in a heavy hallucination, which has nothing to do with reality. What we apprehend has nothing in the slightest to do with reality.

For example, we label "table" on this object that performs the function of supporting things. Mainly because of this function, in dependence upon this function, we label this particular shape "table." However, wherever we point, that is not the table. Each part, each piece of wood—the top, the bottom, the four legs—is not the table; even the whole thing, all the parts together, which performs the function of supporting things, is not the table. The whole group of the parts is not the table—that is the base.

So, the table cannot be found on this anywhere; there is no table on this. But there *is* a table, in dependence on the base. There is a table here. There is no table that can be found on this base, but there is a table here, because there is the base. It is just that there is no table that can be pointed to and found on this base.

Again, the way the table exists in reality is completely different from the way we normally think of its existence. What appears to us and what we apprehend have nothing to do with the reality of the table. The reality is completely something else. When we analyze what the table is, trying to see the reality of the table, how it actually exists, we discover that the table is something other than what we normally think of as a table. Now, from this you can see the hallucination. Table is merely imputed, merely a concept, in the sense that it has no existence from its own side. On this base there is no table, but there is a table here, because there is the base. The table exists in dependence upon the base. Table is simply an idea; I is simply an idea; the aggregates are simply an idea.

Now the lights have gone out. This is a very good example of true existence: truly existent darkness, unlabeled darkness, darkness from its own side. This is a very good example of the object to be refuted. Light, darkness. There is light from its own side, then suddenly there is darkness from its own side. Even though in reality the darkness exists as a mere imputation, it does not appear to us like this. Like the table, like Lama Zopa, when the darkness is suddenly experienced, it appears to be truly existent.

Look at the whole of existence in the same way. Everything is like this: your own I, aggregates, sense objects, samsara, nirvana. The way in which everything—subject, action, object, all the six sense objects—actually exists is very subtle.

THE BASE IS NOT THE LABEL

Look at the nature of everything in this way. The label is imputed to the base, and in turn, that base is also labeled on another base. By nature, everything is merely imputed. In this way, everything is like an illusion. Nothing exists from its own side, but everything appears as if it does.

We label "aggregates" on the base because the base is something that is not the aggregates. First you think of the reason, then a particular label is given by the mind; otherwise, without the reason, there is no way to apply the label. With the five aggregates, first you think of the reasons, the characteristics and functions of each aggregate; then you label "form" on the one that has color and shape and is tangible. In a similar way, you label feeling, recognition, compounded aggregates, and consciousness.

Take consciousness, for example. Because of its function of thinking of an object's meaning and of distinguishing it from other objects, that particular phenomenon is labeled "consciousness" or "mind." The phenomenon that performs such functions as remembering contact with sense objects (through seeing, hearing, and so on), carrying imprints, and continuing from one life to another is labeled "consciousness."

Or, before you label "this is my father" on one person in a group of people, you think of the reasons: the particular shape of his body, his function in relation to you. By remembering the woman who has a particular body shape and a particular relationship to you, amongst hundreds of people, you label that particular shape "mother." It is the same when you say, "this is my enemy" and "this is my friend."

We can also look at our problems in this way. Without someone first labeling "this is AIDS" and then believing in the label, there was no AIDS. Labeling alone is not enough; there has to be belief in the label. Before the particular doctor first gave that label "AIDS" and believed in it, there was no AIDS. Then other people believed in that doctor's label; they also labeled "AIDS" and believed in that label. This is simply what AIDS is.

Just as the base of the table, its parts, is not the table, and the aggregates are not the person, the illness is not AIDS. If that illness is AIDS, why do we need to call it AIDS on top of that? Why do we need to label "AIDS" on AIDS? There is no reason to label "table" on the table. For there to be a purpose to label "table," you have to label "table" on something that is not table. In other words, if the base is table, why should you label "table" on the table? It's only duplicating.

Whenever we label anything, we label on something that is not that label—otherwise it doesn't make any sense. Take a child who is called Behram Singh. The base is the child's aggregates, the association of body and mind. If those aggregates are already Behram Singh, why did the parents have to give them a name? Why did the parents have to decide a name to give? Why did they have to think of and give the name "Behram Singh"? If the base is Behram Singh, why did the parents have to give a name at all? There would be no point if a name is already there. The parents give the name "Behram Singh" because the base is not Behram Singh. This is the reason they label "Behram Singh" on that base.

If the base itself, this place where these Dharma teachings are being given, were Root Institute, there would be no need to give the name "Root Institute" to it. One names "Root Institute" on the base that is not Root Institute. It is the same with AIDS. The base, the illness, is not AIDS; it is the base. So, what is AIDS? AIDS is the label. The label and the base cannot be one. The aggregates and the I are not one; they are different. They are not separate, but they are different; they are not one.

It is the same with AIDS. So, what is AIDS? It is different from the base. In reality, AIDS is *never* the AIDS that one thinks is real from its own side. There is no such AIDS. It is completely empty, existing in mere name. Meditate on the emptiness of cancer and other diseases in the same way.

There is no way for the label to arise without thinking first of the reasons. After seeing a particular form, you then impute a particular label. When we label anything, we think of the characteristics of that object or person, and then we apply the label. The base comes first. We think of or see the base first, then we apply a label to it. This evolution proves that the base is not the label; the label comes later. If the base were the label, it would be crazy to label it again. There would be no reason to label it. You would just be duplicating.

To think about the base and the label as different is another brief way to meditate on emptiness. This is a clear and essential way to get some feeling for emptiness. Practice awareness of this.

EMPTINESS OF THE FIVE AGGREGATES

The aggregates are not the I; the I is nothing other than what is merely imputed to the aggregates. So the I is empty, completely empty. When we say "the aggregates," since the base is not the aggregates, what are the aggregates? The aggregates are nothing other than what is merely imputed, so they are completely empty.

Go through the aggregates one by one. The base on which we label "form" is not form, so what is form? It is nothing other than what is merely imputed. So, form is completely empty.

Then, feeling. The base on which we label "feeling" is not feeling, so what is feeling? It is nothing other than what is merely imputed. So, feeling is completely empty.

Then, recognition. Again, the base on which we label "recognition" is not recognition, so what is recognition? It is nothing other than what is merely imputed.

Then, compounded aggregates. Compounded aggregates comprise all the rest of impermanent phenomena that are not included in the other aggregates of form, feeling, recognition, and consciousness. Phenomena such as the other secondary mental factors, persons, imprints, time, and so forth are included in this category of compounded aggregates.

Again, the base on which we label "compounded aggregates" is not the compounded aggregates, so what are the compounded aggregates? Nothing other than what is merely imputed. So, the compounded aggregates are completely empty.

The base on which we label "consciousness" is not the consciousness, so what is consciousness? The definition I gave before is the base, but the base is not the label "consciousness." To our mind the base and label seem to be mixed, or one. That is the object to be refuted, the object that we have to realize is empty, as it is empty in reality. To our mind, they appear as one. The base and the label don't appear to be different, but in reality they are.

Again, the particular characteristics and functions of the consciousness are the base, so what is consciousness? It is nothing other than what is merely imputed. For example, the I walks, eats, sleeps, sits, builds houses, but this does not mean the I is the aggregates. The same logic can be followed with the consciousness. It performs the function of perceiving objects and so forth, but it is nothing other than what is merely imputed to that particular base with those particular characteristics and functions. Just as the activities of the aggregates are given the label "I am doing this and that," the actions of this particular base are referred to as "consciousness." Just like all of the other aggregates, consciousness is completely empty.

EMPTINESS OF THE SIX SENSE OBJECTS

First, form. Again, the base is not form; form is something different from the base. So, what is it? Again, it is nothing other than what is merely imputed, so form is completely empty. All these things that we call "forms" are completely empty.

For our minds, form cannot be differentiated from the base; it is oneness with the base. If we look at a piece of bamboo, we label "form" on the bamboo, but for us the base, bamboo, and the form cannot be differentiated. We see the base and the form as one, mixed. That is the object to be refuted. We do not recognize the appearance of true existence: we see not simply imputed form but form having existence from its own side.

When we look at and think of the bamboo, to our minds the base and bamboo appear the same. I am not talking about people for whom there is no longer an appearance of true existence; I am talking only of those who do not see the base and bamboo as different. So, that is how the object to be refuted appears.

When we see a form, in reality we see the base; we don't see form, which is the label. The base is not the imputed existent, form. So, what is form? It is nothing other than what is merely imputed; therefore, form is completely empty.

Then, sound. Again there is the base, which we label as interesting sound, uninteresting sound, praise, criticism. Again, the words that we label "sound" are not sound. So, what is sound? It is nothing other than what is merely imputed by the mind. Again, sound is completely empty.

Next, smell. The particular sense object experienced by the nose is labeled "smell." That is the base, not the label "smell." We label "smell" on what the nose experiences, that which is not experienced by the other senses. That is the base, and not the label, the imputed existent, smell. So, what is smell? Smell is nothing other than what is merely imputed by the mind. Again, smell is completely empty.

It is the same with taste. "Taste" is labeled on what the sense of the tongue experiences, that which other senses do not experience. The base itself is not taste, so taste is labeled. So, what is taste? Nothing other than what is merely imputed by the mind; so taste is completely empty.

Touch is the same. "Touch" is labeled on what the physical body experiences through contact, that which is not experienced by the other senses. Again, touch is merely imputed by the mind; therefore, touch is also completely empty.

EMPTINESS OF THE FOUR NOBLE TRUTHS

True suffering—the three types of suffering: suffering of suffering, suffering of change, and pervasive compounded suffering—is merely imputed by the mind. Therefore, true suffering is completely empty. It is as if there is no true suffering.

True cause of suffering is merely imputed to karma and delusions. Therefore, true cause of suffering is completely empty, as if it doesn't exist.

True cessation of suffering, or liberation, in which the mental continuum is purified of all the disturbing-thought obscurations, is nothing other than what is merely imputed by the mind. Therefore, true cessation is completely empty, as if it doesn't exist.

True path is labeled on the wisdom that directly perceives emptiness. Since true path is nothing other than what is merely imputed by the mind, again true path is completely empty of existing from its own side.

All these—true suffering, true cause of suffering, true cessation, and true path—are nothing other than what is merely imputed by the mind; so they are completely empty of existing from their own side.

When you meditate on *The Essence of Wisdom,* go over each aggregate and each sense object. Meditate on each point. Apply the reasoning that each one is empty because it is merely imputed; this will automatically make you feel that it is empty. Concentrate on the emptiness. The more deeply you understand the meaning of merely imputed, of subtle dependent arising, the more deeply you understand emptiness.

This is the way things are. When we practice awareness of this, it is another world. When we are not aware of reality, we live in one world: truly existent I living a truly existent life in a truly existent world. When we don't see reality, we live our life as truly existent I (which doesn't exist), with truly existent aggregates (which don't exist) and truly existent sense objects of form, smell, taste, sound, and touch (which don't exist). We believe in truly existent true suffering (which doesn't exist) and truly existent true cause of suffering (which doesn't exist). We think of real negative karma from its own side (which doesn't exist), real liberation from its own side (which doesn't exist), and the real path that we are meditating upon (which doesn't exist).

BE AWARE OF REALITY ALL THE TIME

The bodhisattva Togme Zangpo says:

> Even though I can sit up here on a throne and talk a lot about emptiness, if someone criticizes or praises me a little, my mind goes crazy. Even though I can say the words "nothing that appears has true existence," like and dislike arise with just a little praise or criticism. Not one single practice can be called the path of the Middle Way.

You may be able to recite by heart and brilliantly explain the whole of Madhyamika—all Nagarjuna's teachings on emptiness, all Lama Tsong Khapa's teachings on greater insight, all the *Perfection of Wisdom* teachings—all the teachings on the Wisdom Gone Beyond. But in daily life if someone says something a little negative or a little positive, offers a little criticism or a little praise, immediately the mind becomes emotional. There is no stability; immediately there is like and dislike. If this is what happens to our mind in daily life, there is not even a particle of practice of right view.

Be aware that all these "real" things that appear to exist from their own side are empty. Understand that they are all hallucinations, which means that they are all empty. In short, all causative phenomena are transitory by nature, and they are empty by nature.

When you do not practice awareness of this in day-to-day life, the mind is overwhelmed by hallucinations, by wrong conceptions, like a city flooded by water. The mind is possessed by wrong thoughts, wrong appearance, wrong view.

As long as the mind is overwhelmed by wrong conceptions, there is no real peace. Life is lived in hallucination. Not seeing everything as illusory is the fundamental hallucination. The people who have not realized emptiness and do not see things as illusory not only see everything as truly existent, which is an illusion, but also experience the basic problem of clinging to everything as if it were true. This wrong conception, this ignorance, is the origin of all the other delusions, which then motivate karma; that karma leaves on the mind the seeds that are the causes of samsara.

Like this, the ignorance believing that everything exists from its own side ties you continuously to samsara, so that from life to life you experience all the three types of suffering. Besides that, it interferes with your achieving liberation and enlightenment, and with your ability to fulfill the wishes of all sentient beings by leading them to the peerless happiness of full enlightenment.

Not the slightest benefit comes from following this ignorance, for you or for others—only harm. Believing this ignorance is completely childish, when in reality no such truly existent phenomena exist. By nature, all phenomena are empty. Everything is without true existence, so it is complete nonsense for your mind to apprehend it as true just because it appears truly existent. This is unnecessary and meaningless, and the shortcomings are infinite. The harm this ignorance causes you is enormous.

There is no reason at all to follow ignorance, which apprehends everything as truly existent and believes in that appearance of true existence. And there is no point at all in allowing discriminating thoughts of attachment and anger to arise.

NO I TO CHERISH

Because in reality the I is completely empty, there is nothing to cherish. Look at the I as empty, then check whether there is any object to cherish. Since the I that exists is merely imputed, there is nothing to cherish, nothing to cling to. If you check, self-cherishing is completely silly, and only creates problems. Although you don't want problems, you create problems.

106

Self-cherishing is a dictatorship. It is a dictatorship meant to benefit the self but one that results in only problems and failure. It is not logical. Check, "Why do I cherish myself? Why do I think that I'm more important than all the numberless other sentient beings? Why do I think I'm so precious?" There is not one valid reason for self-cherishing. Though we can give many reasons why we should cherish others, we cannot find one reason why we should cherish our self.

There is nothing important or precious about the I. Just like you, other sentient beings want happiness and do not want suffering. Others are numberless; you are just one person. Your own self-importance is completely lost when you think of the numberless others. It is nothing. Even if you are born in hell, you are only one person, so there's nothing to be depressed about. Even if you achieve liberation from samsara, you are only one person, so there's no reason to get excited. When you think of the numberless others who, like you, want happiness and do not want suffering, you become completely insignificant.

Therefore, in your life, there is nothing to do other than to work for others, to cherish others. With this attitude, work for other sentient beings with your body, speech, and mind. There is nothing more important in your life than this.

9

Cherishing Others

Real happiness in life starts when you begin to cherish others.

Exchanging Self for Others

*T*HE THOUGHT OF BODHICITTA is unbelievable. It makes everything other than working for sentient beings boring and unsatis-
fying. There is no real interest or enjoyment in life apart from this.
Anything else is meaningless, empty, essenceless.

Real happiness and satisfaction start when you begin to live
your life for others. You retreat for others, practice Dharma for
others, study for others, work in the office for others, cook for
others. When your attitude is transformed so that you do everything for others, to pacify their suffering and obtain their happiness, there is real satisfaction and peace in your heart.

When you are cherishing yourself, thinking only of yourself—
"How can I be happy? How can I be free of problems?"—there is
no happiness in your heart, only worry and fear. You see only problems, and your mind is not relaxed. But in the next moment, when
you change your object of concern to another sentient being—
even if it is only one other sentient being—suddenly your heart is
released from self-cherishing, like limbs released from chains.

As soon as your object of concern changes from yourself to
someone else, your heart is released from the bondage of the self-
cherishing thought. As soon as you change the object of your
cherishing, there is suddenly peace in the very depths of your
heart. Right in the very moment that your mind changes from
self-cherishing to cherishing others, there is liberation, freedom
from the tight bondage of the selfish mind.

Realizing that miserable conditions come from the superstitions
of their own unsubdued minds, Dharma practitioners use these
conditions to destroy their own superstitions. You don't have to
accept what the self-cherishing thought gives you. You can take

the sufferings and problems of others upon yourself. Instead of blaming someone else so that you can feel happy and comfortable, instead of letting someone else experience the suffering, loss, discomfort, unhappiness, hardships, bad reputation, criticism, punishment, or whatever, you take all these difficulties upon yourself and give the victory to the other person. This is the very practical Mahayana teaching of exchanging self for others, renouncing the self and cherishing others.

Here, you give all the problems given to you by your self-cherishing thought back to the self-cherishing thought. Like this, you use your problems to destroy the origin of your sufferings, your own delusions and superstitions. As it says in *Lama Chöpa*:

> Please bless me to see that this chronic disease of cherishing myself is the door to all sufferings, and bless me to put all the blame on the self-cherishing thought in order to destroy the great demon of self-cherishing.

Self-cherishing is the source of all undesirable experiences and obstacles: disease, or failure in business, education, or Dharma practice. Following the self-cherishing thought brings only problems and failure. Instead of blaming some outside condition or harboring in your heart all the harms given by the self-cherishing thought, use them "to destroy the great demon of self-cherishing." Not only do you put all the blame on the self-cherishing thought, but on top of that you even give the problems back to it, using them as the medicine to cure the chronic disease of self-cherishing, superstitions, and delusions.

USING PROBLEMS TO DESTROY SELF-CHERISHING

In order to achieve ultimate happiness, we must destroy our delusions. The Dharma, the path, the Buddha, the guru, for example: all these are meant to destroy your delusions, to hurt your self-cherishing thought and to subdue your mind.

Receiving criticism, disrespect, or bad treatment also hurts your self-cherishing thought, your thought of the eight worldly dharmas. This is not bad, but good. Therefore, hurting your self-cherishing thought and worldly concern is Dharma practice.

Normally in our daily life we interpret someone treating us badly as negative, but actually it is positive. It becomes a remedy for our selfish mind and worldly concern. The person who is treating us badly is helping us to destroy our delusions, our self-cherishing thought, worldly concern, and desire, just like the Dharma does. By doing something opposite to our wish, the person interferes with the comfort we are seeking out of worldly concern, so he or she harms our worldly concern. This is exactly the same as Dharma. Their action becomes the real medicine to cure the real inner disease that we have had from beginningless time—the chronic disease of the three poisonous minds.

It is the same with any problem or miserable condition that you experience, such as having cancer or AIDS, which is the result of having followed the self-cherishing thought and the three poisonous minds in this life or in previous lives. These diseases are not wanted by the self-cherishing thought; again they are like medicine, the path, the Dharma.

Seeing the people who treat you badly or miserable conditions such as disease as negative doesn't help you at all; this only harms you and others. See such people and conditions as positive, as purification. This helps you to exhaust now the heavy negative karma that would otherwise mean your experiencing sufferings in the hells for many hundreds of lifetimes.

Instead of seeing anything that harms your self-cherishing thought and worldly concern as negative, look at it as positive. Use it to destroy your delusions and to achieve liberation and enlightenment. In this way, whether there is a cure for your problem or not—and especially if there is no cure—you can derive benefit from your problem while you are experiencing it.

As mentioned in one thought transformation teaching, "Suffering is a broom that cleans away negative karma and obscurations." Your experiencing problems is the broom, the vacuum cleaner, that cleans away negative karmas, that cleans away the cause of problems.

The teaching also says, "Disease is also a broom that cleans away negative karma and obscurations." Disease is just cited as an example—this can apply to any problem. Life's problems can become the teaching of the Buddha. If you look at problems as positive, you can use them to destroy your self-cherishing thought.

In the practice of *chöd*, you purposely create a terrifying situation and invoke terrifying spirits in order to slay your ego. For the highly realized practitioners who are successful at chöd, it is very easy in such a situation to see clearly the object to be refuted, the truly existent I. The more quickly you recognize it, the more quickly you are able to realize the ultimate nature, the emptiness, of the I, the aggregates, and so forth.

However, you don't have to depend upon chöd to create a situation in which you can try to realize emptiness. Any miserable situation—being ill, being criticized or harmed by someone—is exactly the same. The people who bother you in your everyday life are the same as the spirits you ask to disturb you when you are practicing chöd. Instead of using these difficult people to develop your anger or jealousy and create negative karma, you can use them to recognize the object to be refuted and realize emptiness. You can use the everyday situations that you are already experiencing to realize emptiness and to practice bodhicitta, which means destroying self-cherishing.

Since people who bother you destroy your self-cherishing and other delusions just as the Dharma, the Buddha, and the guru do, they are actually not harming but helping you. Like a mirror, they show you your mistakes and thus help you in the most essential way. By showing you your delusions and helping you to eliminate them, by destroying your delusions and worldly concern in this way, they are giving you ultimate happiness.

By destroying your self-cherishing, these people give you enlightenment, because the main obstacle to achieving enlightenment is the self-cherishing thought. And the main obstacle to achieving liberation is desire, which ties you to samsara. In terms of subduing your mind, the person who destroys your worldly concern is as great and as precious a teacher as Buddha. Through causing you to generate the path within your mind, they make it possible for you to achieve enlightenment. This person is as precious as Buddha, as Dharma.

To be precious and kind like this, the person doesn't have to have a motivation to benefit you. For example, your wisdom realizing emptiness helps you to stop your delusions, but the wisdom realizing emptiness doesn't have any motivation to help you. Medicine is also precious because it cures disease, but it doesn't have any motivation to help.

You do not cherish yourself because you are kind to yourself. That is not your reason. Therefore, cherishing someone else doesn't have to involve their being kind to you either. Why not cherish others in the same way you cherish yourself? Why not cherish your enemy, who helps you to practice Dharma, generate the path, and achieve enlightenment? This person is unbelievably precious, just like guru, Buddha, and Dharma. There are infinite reasons why you should cherish such a person.

OTHERS ARE NUMBERLESS

You are just one person. Even if you are reborn in the hells, you are just one person—nothing much to be depressed about. Even if you achieve liberation from samsara, you are just one person—nothing much to be excited about. All of the numberless sentient beings—those who are called "others"—are just like you in wanting happiness and not wanting suffering. Their wishes are exactly the same as yours, and they are numberless. Each one is as important and as precious as you think you are; and these others, each of whom is so important and so precious, are numberless. You, just one person, are completely insignificant. You are nothing when compared to the numberless others who are so precious and so important. You are nothing precious, nothing important.

If there are two people in addition to you, those two people are greater in number than you and thus more important. It is like the difference between one rupee and two rupees: two rupees is more valuable than one rupee. And 100 rupees is more valuable than one rupee; 1000 rupees is much more valuable than one rupee. Given the choice between taking one rupee or two rupees, you would choose two rupees. If the choice is between one rupee and 100 rupees, of course you would take the 100 rupees. If you had a choice, it would be silly to take the one rupee. You would naturally choose the larger amount. Like this, when you compare yourself with one hundred or one thousand or one million people, or numberless sentient beings, you are nothing precious, nothing important.

Compared to all other human beings, who are uncountable, you are insignificant and unimportant. Also, each of the god, demi-god, animal, preta, and hell realms contains an uncountable number of beings. The number of ants alone is uncountable. So, between you and them, they are more important. In one dark room—even in one corner—there are so many mosquitoes; they are more precious, more important. Think in detail of each realm, of each type of creature. There are so many beings just in the animal realm: butterflies, worms, flies. If you think in detail, it is incredible. Just on this earth, even in one country, there are so many.

Just like you, all these beings want happiness and do not want suffering. There is nothing more important in your life than working for sentient beings: pacifying their suffering and giving them happiness. There is nothing more important than this. Anything other than living your life for other sentient beings is meaningless, empty.

What we call "I" is completely insignificant when compared to the numberless human beings, the numberless animals, and the numberless other sentient beings. Each time that we generate bodhicitta, thinking "I am going to achieve enlightenment for all sentient beings," this includes all those beings, all the mosquitoes and ants. Think of how many suffering creatures, such as worms and flies, there are on one mountain; the bodhicitta we generate includes all of them. It includes all the fish, and all the animals that eat the fish. It includes every single one of the numberless creatures in the water, big and small, that eat each other. Each time that we generate bodhicitta, the altruistic wish to obtain happiness for others, it encompasses without discrimination all the different human races, every type of creature in the water, on the ground, in the air. Without discrimination, it encompasses every living being.

This altruistic thought to achieve enlightenment for all sentient beings is an incredible attitude. When you generate bodhicitta, you include everybody in your thought to benefit. No matter what problem they have, no matter where they are—the East, the West, the Middle East, another world—everybody is included. Not even one sentient being is left out.

WHY WE NEED OMNISCIENT MIND

Each sentient being has a different level of mind and different characteristics, and you have to know the exact method to fit each one. You should be able to say one word at the same time to millions of people and suit each one. Each one will hear something different according to their different level of mind, their different karma; but at the same time, according to their karma, what they hear should guide them on the right path, to liberation and to enlightenment.

However, right now we cannot see even one sentient being's level of mind, one sentient being's karma. To be able to guide all sentient beings perfectly, without the slightest mistake, and benefit them extensively, we need to know everything about each one's level of mind and characteristics.

Also, to lead even one sentient being gradually to enlightenment, we need the foundation of knowing the whole path. We cannot reveal just one method; one method cannot suit everyone. There have to be various methods in accordance with the levels of beings' minds. For example, by telling Ajatashatru (Tibetan, *Makyeda*), who had killed his father and mother, "Father and mother are objects to be killed," Guru Shakyamuni Buddha made him feel happy. In his depression and anxiety, it was helpful for Ajatashatru to hear this. It actually helped him to realize the two selflessnesses, of persons and of aggregates, and to understand that the two ignorances were to be eliminated. These words became the cause for Ajatashatru to actualize emptiness. Instead of getting stuck on the literal meaning, Ajatashatru understood that the words meant that the two types of ignorance, apprehending the I and apprehending the aggregates as truly existent, were to be eliminated.

To say that everything is truly existent suits the minds of some people. Hearing this helps them to practice better and leads them to happiness. Though there is not even one atom of true existence, to that particular person with no capacity to understand that there is no true existence, one would teach that Buddha said there is true existence, because this instruction would become the gradual means to lead that sentient being to liberation and enlightenment.

To lead sentient beings gradually to happiness and enlightenment, one has to see every single karma, every level of mind and characteristic of every sentient being, and all the various methods that are suited to each of them. And that comes only with omniscient mind. Even arhats, who have infinite psychic powers, cannot see every single karma. Though free of disturbing-thought obscurations, arhats have still not removed the subtle obscurations to omniscience, so they cannot see subtle karma or the secret actions of the Buddhas. Arhats cannot perfectly guide sentient beings, even though they themselves are free of samsara.

Therefore, to work perfectly to benefit all sentient beings, one has to achieve the state of omniscient mind— no matter how many eons it takes, no matter how hard it is. There is no other method. Until one achieves omniscient mind, the realizations of one's own mind are not complete, and one cannot give sentient beings what they need, which is the highest, longest-lasting happiness. Achieving enlightenment is the most meaningful thing one can do to benefit oneself and to benefit other sentient beings.

WE ARE RESPONSIBLE FOR ALL SENTIENT BEINGS

You can understand the idea of highest happiness from an everyday example. Given a choice, even animals will choose the most delicious food and leave other food that is not so interesting. Even a dog does this. And when shopping or doing business, people try to get the most profitable deal they can by buying the best quality, longest lasting goods. Even though they may not know that they can achieve such a thing as enlightenment, in our daily lives we all wish to get the best. Unless extremely poor, everyone tries to get the best of everything, to build the best, longest lasting house. Even though there may be no knowledge of enlightenment, there is a concept of peerless happiness. It is only because of lacking the Dharma wisdom-eye that people are not aware that enlightenment is the main thing missing in their lives, and is what they need to achieve.

Just as you are always trying to get the most in terms of happiness, so too is every other sentient being. What everyone needs is the peerless happiness of full enlightenment, the state free of all

119

obscurations and complete in all realizations.

Having received a perfect human rebirth, met a virtuous teacher to lead us on the path to liberation and enlightenment, and met the Buddhadharma—especially the Mahayana teachings—each of us has the opportunity to free all sentient beings from all obscurations and sufferings and lead them to the fully enlightened state. We have this opportunity to help because we have received all the necessary conditions to develop our mind, to generate the graduated path to enlightenment, and to achieve omniscient mind, which has great compassion for all sentient beings and the capacity to guide them. Therefore, we are responsible for freeing all sentient beings from all suffering and its causes, the obscurations, and for leading them to the fully enlightened state.

I often use this example: If you saw a blind person walking towards a cliff, you would immediately grab them before they fell over the precipice. It wouldn't matter whether they asked for help or not. If you have all the necessary conditions—eyes to see, limbs to grab, voice to call—then you are capable of helping the blind person. Simply by having these, you are responsible for helping the person who is in danger of falling off the cliff.

If someone who had the capacity to help saw the situation and didn't lend a hand, it would be very cruel and shameful. Somehow it wouldn't fulfill the purpose of having eyes and limbs, which is to use them to help others. If such a thing happened, how pitiful it would be from the side of the blind person about to fall off the cliff, and how terrible from the side of the person who had all the conditions necessary to help, but didn't.

How very cruel and harmful it would be, if now while we have all the necessary conditions, we don't practice bodhicitta, the essence of Buddha's teachings, especially the Mahayana teachings; if we don't develop this ultimate good heart; if we don't develop the capacity to guide sentient beings; if we don't achieve enlightenment in order to work perfectly for sentient beings, but instead always live with the self-cherishing thought, thinking of nothing but our own happiness. How selfish and cruel this would be. In reality, we are completely responsible for leading all sentient beings to enlightenment.

SACRIFICING YOURSELF

Concern for other sentient beings brings a natural wish to give them happiness and not harm them. You don't want to lead them to suffering. Remember the story of the bodhisattva captain who, by killing that one person who was planning to kill the five hundred traders, sacrificed himself completely. In order to save that person from creating negative karma, the bodhisattva captain was willing to be reborn in the hells. But instead of becoming negative karma and the cause of rebirth in the lower realms, his action of killing shortened his time in samsara by 100,000 eons. By generating bodhicitta and cherishing this one sentient being, by exchanging himself for this one sentient being, the bodhisattva captain accumulated incredible merit and came closer to enlightenment.

There is also a story about Asanga. For twelve years he tried to achieve Maitreya Buddha in his meditations, but for all those years he was unable to see Maitreya Buddha. One day when Asanga was returning to his cave, he saw a wounded dog full of maggots. He felt such unbearable compassion. First he cut flesh from his own leg and spread it out on the ground so that he could put the maggots from the dog's body onto it. And then, so as not to kill the maggots by removing them with his fingers, he bent down to pick them up with the tip of his tongue. As he leaned forward to do this, with his eyes closed, he found that he could not reach the dog. Asanga opened his eyes and saw Maitreya Buddha right there, instead of the dog. Sacrificing himself for what he saw as a wounded dog became powerful purification;

only after this did Asanga see Maitreya Buddha.

There are many other stories like this. Sacrificing yourself to protect even one sentient being from suffering and lead them to happiness is powerful purification. Not only does it purify many eons of negative karma, but it accumulates much merit, bringing you closer to enlightenment. The fact that you can achieve enlightenment quickly by sacrificing yourself for even one sentient being is one reason to cherish others.

Cherishing yourself is an obstacle to the development of the mind, to the generation of realizations of the path. If you cherish yourself, there is no enlightenment, but if you cherish even one sentient being, there is enlightenment. Cherishing even one sentient being makes possible the achievement of enlightenment.

So there is a big difference. With the self-cherishing thought, there is no hope of enlightenment; but cherishing one sentient being, which purifies obscurations and accumulates extensive merit, leads you to enlightenment. From these stories and reasons, the conclusion is that even one sentient being is much more precious than you. Without considering how precious sentient beings are due to their great number, you can see that even one sentient being is unbelievably precious. There is no way to finish explaining the value of this sentient being, all the benefits you can gain from this one sentient being.

What is called "I" is the object to be abandoned forever; what is called "others"—even one sentient being—is the object to be cherished forever. This is why living your life for others—dedicating your life to even one sentient being—gives the greatest enjoyment and the most interesting life. Real happiness in life starts when you cherish others. Living your life for others, cherishing them with loving kindness and compassion, is the door to happiness, the door to enlightenment.

10

Having No Choice
But to Practice Dharma

Since you don't like problems, there is no choice:
you have to practice Dharma.

*H*IS HOLINESS THE DALAI LAMA often advises that the best way to live one's life is in an isolated solitary place, renouncing this life and the eight worldly dharmas, and one-pointedly concentrating the mind on the graduated path to enlightenment. Developing realizations of the path to enlightenment is the best. But not everybody can do this.

For those who cannot live such a life but who have a Dharma education, the second best choice is to teach Dharma to others. Even though such people cannot practice complete renunciation, they practice as much as they can and teach others. For those who don't have the Dharma education needed to teach others, the third option is to practice as much as possible and to serve others in society.

There is no choice. Since you don't like problems, there is no choice: you have to practice Dharma. This is the conclusion. Dharma is the only means to stop problems and to bring peace in the mind. There is nothing else. If you don't like suffering, there is no way to escape from Dharma practice. Practicing Dharma means renouncing the causes of problems, which are in your mind, and creating the causes of happiness, which are also in your mind.

All the problems of this life and of future lives come from non-virtuous karma and the self-cherishing thought, and from the root, the self-grasping thought, the ignorance that grasps the I as truly existent. If you want to stop experiencing problems now and in the future, you have to purify the negative karma already created and abandon creating further negative karma. That is Dharma practice. That is how you solve life's problems.

For example, one may have a serious disease that cannot be cured by any common external treatment. This means the obstacle is very great, and often one can recover only by doing very intensive, prolonged Dharma practice. If one has the karma to meet a lama who can give the correct advice on Dharma practice and meditation instructions, one can then recover. There are many examples of people with illnesses who were not helped by taking medicines over a long period but who recovered by practicing Dharma. People have recovered from cancer by doing meditation.

One of my uncles, for example, was sick for many years. Even though he went to Tibet and saw many doctors, nothing helped. Finally, he went to see one meditator who lived in Charok, near Lawudo Cave, where I go sometimes. This meditator advised my uncle that since his illness was due to his karmic obscurations, he needed to do a lot of purification. My uncle then received instructions on the preliminary practices—prostrations, refuge, and so forth—from that lama and also from another old lama who is still living at Charok.

While doing the preliminary practices, my uncle gradually recovered from his disease. He did 700,000 prostrations. At the same time he also took care of my grandmother, who was blind. He would bring food to her, take her outside to the toilet, bring her back inside, and all these things. For many years he took care of her.

There are many stories like this. When external means cannot help our present problem, again we have to take refuge in Dharma. We have to practice Dharma, not only to avoid the experience of problems in future lives, but also to stop our present problems. The conclusion is that we have to practice Dharma.

Whether you are Buddhist or non-Buddhist, there is no other way to solve life's problems and to make it impossible for them to occur again. No matter how many problems you experience, you have to practice Dharma. Even though you may not have time to do long retreats or study extensively, you have to do what you can to practice Dharma, because you don't want problems and unhappiness. Even though you may have many problems with disease or with your relationships, you cannot use this as an excuse to give up practicing Dharma. You have to do what you can; you have to practice Dharma.

Even though you don't have the karma now to live an ascetic life like some meditators, renouncing this life, it is important to generate the wish to do so. Don't think, "I cannot live like that, so what's the purpose of listening to this teaching?" There are many benefits. Even though you cannot practice now, generating the wish to be able to practice in the future is the seed that makes it possible later to actually be able to practice pure Dharma, to live an ascetic life, to renounce the eight worldly dharmas. In this way, you will be able to succeed in actualizing the path to enlightenment.

It is very important to read the lam-rim. Even though you may study *Madhyamakavatara, Abhisamayalankara,* and other philosophical texts extensively, unless you pay attention to the lam-rim, you won't know the meaning of worldly dharma. Unless you are aware of texts such as *Opening the Door of Dharma,* which give instruction on this very simple initial Dharma practice, you will make the mistake of thinking that only a few actions are worldly activity. Being aware of this instruction is so useful for our practice.

In each day we have so many opportunities to practice renunciation, accumulate merit, and achieve enlightenment. Each day we can accumulate so much merit when we do our deity practices. There are so many things involved: the motivation at the beginning, the offerings, generating out of emptiness as the deity. We accumulate so much merit doing even one sadhana.

Meditating on emptiness for even one second purifies the heavy negative karma of the ten non-virtuous actions. It is said that merely wishing to meditate on emptiness purifies those negative karmas and accumulates much merit. Just having the wish to hear the *Prajnaparamita* teachings purifies many eons of heavy negative karma that one has accumulated in past lives. Also, as mentioned in *A Guide to the Bodhisattva's Way of Life*, meditating on bodhicitta has infinite benefits in terms of purification; it is one of the most powerful means of purification. And in terms of accumulating extensive merit, bodhicitta is the most skillful method.

I think the Dharma practices explained in *Opening the Door of Dharma* are very important. They are the main refuge in life and are extremely effective for the mind. They help to stop every kind of problem. Reading, thinking about, and especially practicing *Opening the Door of Dharma* is the solution to problems.

For lay people, this text outlines the psychology needed to solve problems, especially at those times that you feel your life has become hell; when you experience such misery that you want to commit suicide. As lay people, you cannot dedicate your whole life to following desire. Life becomes too much. You will be constantly unhappy if you leave everything up to desire and worldly concern. This only makes life extremely miserable for you, and for others. Even before being born in hell, you create another type of hell for yourself in the human realm. And not only are you yourself miserable but you bring so many other beings into hell; you cause others so many problems.

Of course, there is no question that Dharma practice is the real refuge in life. Thought training helps to bring not only peace in your own mind, but peace in the minds of many other people. When you are peaceful and harmonious, you do not interfere with others' lives and practice. Thought training is also very important for anyone who wants to practice lam-rim, because without it there is no development of the path to enlightenment. With thought training, which cuts off worldly concern, development of the mind in the lam-rim path comes automatically. I think it is especially important for anyone who does retreat, whether short or long. Thought training is an excellent support for retreat. By helping to keep the mind quiet and to stop obstacles, it enables the retreat to become successful.

For monks and nuns, I think thought training is the fundamental practice. Without this practice, one cannot continue ordained life; one finds it difficult to continue the practice of morality. Not only that, this practice is one of the main supports of developing the mind, of actualizing the lam-rim path. Especially for monks and nuns, this teaching is the foundation of the practice, to be heard and read again and again, and remembered. This is the real refuge, the real protection.

The conclusion is, it is extremely important to practice Dharma, which means not allowing delusions to overwhelm you completely. No matter how many problems and difficulties you have, you still need to practice Dharma. You have to practice; you have to try. By controlling desire once, twice, three times, four times in one day, you do not create that negative karma, and you do not allow all the other negative thoughts to arise. You need to practice Dharma, even for peace in your life from moment to moment. Meditate on impermanence and death as the foundation, then train your mind in the lam-rim. Attempt to accumulate merit and purify negative karma as much as possible.

MAKING THE DETERMINATION TO PRACTICE

Even when we find time to do some Dharma activity, it is the thought of the eight worldly dharmas that does not allow our practice to become pure Dharma. Because it causes laziness, this thought makes us unable to practice Dharma, or delays our practice. It weakens our mind so that we are unable to make a determination to practice.

The whole thing is a question of determination. Without determination, development doesn't come. My first alphabet teacher, whose holy name was Aku Lekshe, whom I have already mentioned, used to tell me that the whole problem is being unable to make the determination to practice Dharma. He taught me this the very first time he taught me the alphabet; and the last time we were together, before he passed away, he was still saying this when he talked about Dharma.

This inability to make the determination becomes the source of problems and obstacles. Your own mind creates the difficulty. Your own mind makes it difficult to practice and to generate the realizations of the path. If the determination to practice is made, there are no difficulties; if the determination is not made, there are. There are no difficulties from the side of Dharma, from the side of the path. There are no external difficulties. Difficulty in practicing Dharma comes from your own mind, from your inability to make the necessary determination. And what makes you unable to make that determination is the thought of the eight worldly dharmas.

When you separate yourself from the evil thought of the eight worldly dharmas, there are no difficulties in your practice. When you live inseparably with this thought, when you are a friend of the eight worldly dharmas, there are difficulties. There is no Dharma that is difficult from its own side; there is no truly existent difficulty. Your own mind creates the difficulty. There is no difficulty apart from your inability to make the determination to practice.

If you are able to make the determination to not follow desire and to practice Dharma right now, there is peace; if you cannot, there is no peace. On this very seat, in this very minute that you make the determination, immediately there is peace. When you do not make this determination, there is no peace. If you make the determination, peace is something that you can experience immediately, right in this second. There is no other choice; there is no other solution.

11

Dedicating the Merits

*Dedicating merit with bodhicitta
is like putting a drop of water into an ocean:
as long as the ocean exists, the drop exists.*

Dedicating with Bodhicitta

*D*EDICATE THAT BY HEARING each word of these teachings, you may be able to realize immediately the whole path to enlightenment, especially bodhicitta. Also pray that each word of these teachings be able to subdue immediately the minds of all sentient beings; that the whole path to enlightenment, especially bodhicitta, be generated in their minds.

In *A Guide to the Bodhisattva's Way of Life,* the great bodhisattva Shantideva says:

> All other virtues are like the banana tree: the fruit comes, and the tree finishes. But the tree of bodhicitta gives fruit unceasingly.

Dedicating merit just to achieve the happiness of future lives or self-liberation is essenceless compared to dedicating the merit with bodhicitta to achieve enlightenment. Dedicating merit with bodhicitta is like putting a drop of water into an ocean: as long as the ocean exists, the drop exists. If we dedicate with bodhicitta, however small the merit we accumulate, it becomes inexhaustible. We experience the result of this merit unceasingly until we achieve enlightenment. After achieving enlightenment through this, we can then gradually lead all other sentient beings to enlightenment.

We *must* dedicate for the generation of bodhicitta. This is why at the end of every teaching we recite:

> *jang-chub sem-chog rin-po-che*
> *ma-kye-pa-nam kye-gyur-chig*
> *kye-pa nyam-pa me-pa-yang*
> *gong-ne gong-du pel-war shog*

May the precious bodhicitta not yet generated, be
generated,
And may that generated never degenerate but always
increase.

It is very important to dedicate to generate bodhicitta, which is
the source of all happiness for you and for others. It is one of the
practices of the five powers: the power of prayer. Bodhicitta is the
door to all success, preventing all undesirable things and bringing
all desirable things. Bodhicitta fulfills all your wishes and the
wishes of others. Therefore, it is very important to dedicate to
generate bodhicitta in your own mind and in the minds of others, and for those who have already generated bodhicitta to
increase it.

DEDICATING WITH EMPTINESS

In addition to dedicating merit to achieve enlightenment, seal it
with emptiness by thinking that the one who dedicates the merit,
the action of dedicating, and the object of dedication are all
empty. In this way the merit cannot be destroyed by anger or
heresy. Anger and heresy not only result in rebirth in the lower
realms but also delay the achievement of realizations for thousands of eons.

As Geshe Sopa Rinpoche has said, the merit sealed with emptiness cannot be harmed by anger or heresy because anger and
heresy arise from the ignorance that grasps true existence, which
is eliminated by the wisdom that realizes emptiness. Because the
wisdom realizing emptiness eliminates the root of the delusions,
the ignorance grasping at true existence, merit cannot be harmed
by anger or heresy if it is sealed with emptiness.

If you have no idea of emptiness, of subtle dependent arising,
Pabongka Dechen Nyingpo advises that at the very least you
should think that you are dreaming, that you are dedicating the

merit in a dream. In this way you do not grasp the I, the merit, sentient beings, and enlightenment as truly existent. This grasping is lessened. Apprehending everything in this way, as if in a dream, gives you the idea that this is not a real I, a truly existent I, an I from its own side. It gives you a rough idea that all these are false, that there is no existence from its own side. With this awareness, dedicate the merit.

Otherwise, if you have some understanding of emptiness, remember the subtle reality of how everything exists. Remember that the I who dedicates is merely imputed, the action is merely imputed, enlightenment is merely imputed, and the sentient beings for whom we dedicate the merit are also merely imputed. When you think of enlightenment, the understanding in your heart should be that it is nothing other than what is merely imputed. And that which brings the result of happiness, which we call "merit," is also merely imputed. Therefore all these—I, action of dedicating, merit, enlightenment—are completely empty.

With this subtle awareness, looking at everything as completely empty, and with the thought of bodhicitta, dedicate the merits of having listened to these teachings.

Glossary

(Skt = Sanskrit; Tib = Tibetan)

Abhisamayalankara (Skt). *Ornament for Clear Realization,* by Maitreya; a philosophical text studied in Tibetan monasteries, which covers subjects such as emptiness, the qualities of a Buddha, and all the stages of the path to Buddhahood.

aggregates. The association of body and mind; a person comprises five aggregates: form, feeling, recognition, compounded aggregates, and consciousness.

arhat (Skt). Literally, "foe destroyer." A being who has destroyed his or her delusions and attained liberation from cyclic existence.

Aryadeva. The chief disciple of Nagarjuna and a leading proponent of the Prasangika-Madhyamika school of Buddhist tenets.

Asanga. The fifth-century Indian pandit who founded the Cittamatra (Mind Only) school of Buddhist tenets.

Baudhanath. A village just outside Kathmandu that is built around the Baudhanath Stupa, a famous Buddhist pilgrimage site.

bodhicitta (Skt). The altruistic aspiration to achieve enlightenment in order to enlighten all living beings.

bodhisattva (Skt). One who possesses bodhicitta.

Brahma. A powerful Hindu deity in the god realm.

137

Buddha (Skt). A fully enlightened being. (See *enlightenment.*)

Buddhadharma (Skt). See *Dharma.*

Buddha-nature. Refers to the emptiness, or ultimate nature, of the mind. Because of this nature, every sentient being possesses the potential to become fully enlightened, a Buddha.

causal path. Another term for Paramitayana (q.v.). In following this path, one accumulates merit for many eons, thus creating the cause for the ultimate goal of enlightenment.

causative phenomena. Things that come about in dependence upon causes and conditions; includes all objects experienced by the senses, as well as the mind itself; impermanent phenomena.

Chenrezig (Tib). Or, in Sanskrit, Avalokiteshvara; Buddha of Compassion; the male meditational deity that embodies fully enlightened compassion. The Dalai Lamas are said to be emanations of this deity.

chöd (Tib). A tantric practice aimed at destroying self-grasping, often performed in frightening surroundings, such as charnel grounds.

chuba (Tib). The traditional outer garment worn by Tibetans, both male and female. The male version has long sleeves.

clear light. The ever-present subtlest state of mind, achieved when all the energy-winds have dissolved into the central channel, as happens, for example, during death; it is utilized in meditation by accomplished tantric practitioners; the cause of the dharmakaya.

completion stage. The second of the two stages of Highest Yoga Tantra, during which control is gained over the subtle mind and body through such practices as inner fire.

creative bodhicitta. The simulated bodhicitta that one generates prior to the actual effortless attainment of bodhicitta.

cyclic existence. See *samsara.*

delusions. The negative states of mind that are the cause of suffering. The three root delusions are ignorance, anger, and attachment.

Devadatta. Shakyamuni Buddha's cousin who was jealous of Buddha and constantly tried to harm him.

Dharma (Skt). In general, spiritual practice; specifically, the Buddhist teachings; Buddhadharma.

dharmakaya (Skt). The omniscient mind of a Buddha.

disturbing thoughts. See *delusions.*

disturbing-thought obscurations. The delusions, which obstruct the attainment of liberation.

Domo Geshe Rinpoche. A famous ascetic meditator in his early life who later established monastic communities in the Tibet-Nepal border area and in Darjeeling. He passed away in 1936. (One of his disciples was the German, Lama Govinda, who wrote about him in his book, *The Way of the White Clouds*.) His reincarnation now lives in the United States.

Drepung Monastery. Founded near Lhasa in 1416 by one of Lama Tsong Khapa's disciples and the largest of the three major Gelug monasteries. A Drepung in exile has been established in South India.

Dromtönpa (1005–1064). A Tibetan layman, Dromtönpa was

Lama Atisha's translator and heart disciple; propagator of the Kadam tradition.

eight freedoms. The eight states from which a perfect human rebirth is free: (1) being born in a hell realm; (2) being born as a hungry ghost; (3) being born as an animal; (4) being born as a long-life god; (5) being born as a barbarian; (6) holding wrong views; (7) being born in a dark age when no Buddha has descended; (8) being born with defective mental or physical faculties.

eight worldly dharmas. The worldly concerns that generally motivate the actions of ordinary beings: (1) being happy when acquiring something; (2) being unhappy when not acquiring something; (3) wanting to be happy; (4) not wanting to be unhappy; (5) wanting to hear interesting sounds; (6) not wanting to hear uninteresting sounds; (7) wanting praise; (8) not wanting criticism.[Sometimes (5) and (6) are explained as wanting fame and not wanting notoriety, respectively. (Pabongka Rinpoche, *Liberation in the Palm of Your Hand*, p. 335.)]

emptiness. The absence, or lack of, true existence. Ultimately, every phenomenon is empty of existing truly, or from its own side, or independently. (See *merely labeled*.)

enlightenment. Buddhahood; omniscience; full awakening; the ultimate goal of Mahayana Buddhist practice, attained when all limitations have been removed from the mind and all positive potential has been realized; a state characterized by unlimited compassion, skill, and wisdom.

The Essence of Wisdom. Also known as *The Heart Sutra*. Recited daily by many Buddhist practitioners, it is one of the shortest of the *Perfection of Wisdom* texts.

five types of knowledge. The five major sciences studied in Tibetan Buddhist monasteries: grammar, logic, medicine, arts and crafts, and religious philosophy.

five precepts. The vows taken by lay Buddhist practitioners: no killing, no stealing, no lying, no sexual misconduct, and no intoxicants.

five uninterrupted negative karmas. Killing one's father, one's mother, or an arhat; maliciously drawing blood from a Buddha; causing a schism within the Sangha.

four elements. Earth, water, fire, and air, or wind.

four noble truths. The subject of the Buddha's first discourse: true suffering, true cause of suffering, true cessation of suffering, and true path to the cessation of suffering.

Ganden Monastery. Situated 55 km east of Lhasa, the first of the three great Gelug monastic universities in Lhasa, it was founded in 1409 by Lama Tsong Khapa. A Ganden in exile has been established in South India.

Gelug (Tib). The Virtuous Order; the order of Tibetan Buddhism founded by Lama Tsong Khapa and his disciples in the early fifteenth century.

generation stage. The first of the two stages of Highest Yoga Tantra, during which one cultivates the clear appearance and divine pride of oneself as a meditational deity.

geshe (Tib). Literally, "virtuous spiritual friend." A term given to the great Kadampas; the title conferred on those who have completed extensive studies and examinations at Gelug monastic universities.

graduated path to enlightenment. Or, in Tibetan, lam-rim. Originally outlined in Tibet by Lama Atisha in *Lamp on the Path to Enlightenment,* the graduated path is a step-by-step presentation of Buddha's teachings.

Great Vehicle. See *Mahayana.*

Guhyasamaja (Skt). A male meditational deity of Highest Yoga Tantra.

Guru Shakyamuni Buddha (563–483 BC). The fourth of the one thousand Buddhas of this present world age, he was born a prince of the Shakya clan in North India and taught the sutra and tantra paths to liberation and full enlightenment.

happy migratory being. A samsaric being in the realms of gods, demi-gods, or humans.

hell being. A samsaric being in the realm of greatest suffering.

Hinayana (Skt).The Lesser Vehicle; the path of the arhats, the ultimate goal of which is nirvana.

His Holiness Ling Rinpoche (1903–1983). The Senior Tutor of His Holiness the Fourteenth Dalai Lama and Ninety-seventh Ganden Throneholder, head of the Gelug order.

His Holiness Serkong Rinpoche (1914–1983). A master debate partner of His Holiness the Fourteenth Dalai Lama.

His Holiness Song Rinpoche (1905–1984). A powerful lama renowned for his wrathful aspect who had impeccable knowledge of Tibetan Buddhist rituals, art, and science.

hungry ghost. See *preta.*

illusory body. A subtle bodily form generated through the practice of the completion stage of Highest Yoga Tantra; the cause of the rupakaya.

imprint. The seed, or potential, left on the mind by positive or negative actions of body, speech, and mind.

Indra. A powerful Hindu deity in the god realm.

inner fire. Or, in Tibetan, tum-mo; the energy residing at the navel chakra, aroused during the completion stage of Highest Yoga Tantra.

Istituto Lama Tzong Khapa. A Buddhist center in Italy founded by Lama Thubten Yeshe and Lama Thubten Zopa Rinpoche.

Kadampa geshe. A practitioner of the Buddhist tradition that originated in Tibet in the eleventh century with the teachings of Atisha. Kadampa geshes are renowned for their practice of thought transformation.

Kalachakra (Skt). Literally, "cycle of time." A male meditational deity of Highest Yoga Tantra.

Kangyur (Tib). The part of the Tibetan Buddhist canon that contains the discourses attributed to Shakyamuni Buddha.

karma (Skt). Literally, "action." The law of cause and effect: the process whereby virtuous actions of body, speech, and mind lead to happiness and non-virtuous ones to suffering.

Kirti Tsenshab Rinpoche (b. 1926). An ascetic meditator and a principal holder of the Kalachakra lineage.

Kopan. The monastery founded in 1969 by Lama Thubten Yeshe and Lama Thubten Zopa Rinpoche near Baudhanath in the Kathmandu valley, Nepal.

lama (Tib). Or, in Sanskrit, guru; spiritual teacher, master; literally, "heavy," as in heavy with Dharma knowledge.

Lama Atisha (982–1054). The renowned Indian Buddhist master who came to Tibet to help in the revival of Buddhism and established the Kadam tradition. His text *Lamp on the Path to Enlightenment* was the first lam-rim text.

Lama Chöpa (Tib). Or, in Sanskrit, *Guru Puja*; an extensive practice involving prayers, requests, and offerings to the lama.

lam-rim (Tib). See *graduated path to enlightenment.*

Lawudo Cave. The cave in the Solu Khumbu region of Nepal where the Lawudo Lama lived and meditated for many years. Lama Zopa Rinpoche is recognized as the reincarnation of the Lawudo Lama.

liberation. The state of complete liberation from samsara; nirvana, the state beyond sorrow; the goal of the Hinayana practitioner.

lineage lamas. The spiritual teachers who constitute the line of direct guru-disciple transmission of teachings, from Buddha to the teachers of the present day.

lower realms. The three realms of cyclic existence with the most suffering: the hell, preta, and animal realms. (See *samsara.*)

Lower Tantric College. Or, in Tibetan, Gyu-me; the tantric college, originally in lower Lhasa, that has now been reestablished in India; one of the two main Gelug colleges that specialize in the study of tantric rituals.

lung disease. Literally, air, or wind, disease; the state in which the wind element within the body is unbalanced.

Madhyamakavatara (Skt). *Supplement to (Nagarjuna's) "Treatise on the Middle Way,"* by the seventh-century Indian master Chandrakirti; one of the philosophical texts studied in Tibetan monasteries.

Madhyamika (Skt). The Middle Way. A philosophical system founded by Nagarjuna, based on the *Perfection of Wisdom Sutras* of Shakyamuni Buddha, and considered to be the supreme presentation of Buddha's teachings on emptiness.

Mahakala (Skt). A wrathful tantric deity.

Mahayana (Skt). The Great Vehicle; the path of the bodhisattvas, the ultimate goal of which is Buddhahood. It includes both Paramitayana and Vajrayana.

Maitreya Buddha (Skt). The Loving One. The next Buddha, after Shakyamuni, and fifth of the thousand Buddhas of this present world age.

mala (Skt). A rosary used for counting mantras.

mantra (Skt). Literally, "protection of the mind." Sanskrit syllables recited in conjunction with the practice of a particular meditational deity and embodying the qualities of that deity.

merely labeled. The subtlest meaning of dependent arising; every phenomenon exists relatively, or conventionally, as a mere label, as merely imputed by the mind. (See *emptiness.*)

merit. The positive energy accumulated in the mind as a result of virtuous actions of body, speech, and mind.

Middle Way. See *Madhyamika.*

migratory beings. Another term for sentient beings, who migrate from rebirth to rebirth within the six realms of samsara.

migtsema (Tib). A verse of praise recited during the practice of the Lama Tsong Khapa Guru Yoga.

Milarepa (1040–1123). The great ascetic Tibetan yogi and poet, foremost disciple of Marpa, famous for his intense practice, devotion to his guru, his many songs of spiritual realization, and his attainment of enlightenment in one lifetime.

Nagarjuna. The great Indian scholar and tantric adept who lived approximately four hundred years after Buddha's death. Propounder of the Middle Way, he clarified the ultimate meaning of Buddha's teachings on emptiness.

nirvana (Skt). See *liberation.*

non-abiding sorrowless state. See *enlightenment.*

Nyingma (Tib). The oldest of the four orders of Tibetan Buddhism, which traces its teachings back to Padmasambhava, the eighth-century Indian yogi. (The other orders are Sakya, Kagyu, and Gelug.)

obscurations to omniscience. The subtle defilements of the mind that obstruct the attainment of enlightenment.

om mani padme hung. The mantra of Chenrezig, Buddha of Compassion.

omniscient mind. See *enlightenment.*

Pabongka Dechen Nyingpo (1871–1941). An influential and powerful lama of the Gelug order, Pabongka Rinpoche was the root guru of His Holiness the Dalai Lama's Senior and Junior Tutors.

Padmasambhava. The eighth-century Indian tantric master mainly responsible for the establishment of Buddhism in Tibet, revered by all Tibetan Buddhists, especially the Nyingmapas.

pandit (Skt). A highly learned philosopher.

paramitas (Skt). Or perfections; the practices of a bodhisattva. On the basis of bodhicitta, a bodhisattva practices the six paramitas: generosity, ethics, patience, enthusiastic perseverance, concentration, and wisdom.

Paramitayana (Skt). Literally, "Perfection Vehicle"; the part of the Mahayana that does not include tantra.

path of preparation. The second of the five paths leading to Buddhahood. The five are: accumulation, preparation, seeing, meditation, and no more learning.

path of seeing. The third of the five paths to Buddhahood.

patience level. The third of the four divisions of the path of seeing.

perfect human rebirth. See *precious human body.*

Perfection of Wisdom. Or, in Sanskrit, *Prajnaparamita*; the teachings of Shakyamuni Buddha in which the wisdom of emptiness and the path of the bodhisattva are explained.

perfections. See *paramitas.*

pervasive compounded suffering. The most subtle of the three types of suffering, it refers to the nature of the five aggregates, contaminated by karma and delusions.

Prajnaparamita (Skt). See *Perfection of Wisdom*. Also the name of the female deity that embodies wisdom.

Prasangika-Madhyamika (Skt). The Middle Way Consequence School; considered to be the highest of all Buddhist philosophical tenets.

precious human body. The rare human state, qualified by the eight freedoms and ten richnesses, that is the ideal condition for practicing Dharma and achieving enlightenment.

preliminary practices. The meditations for removing hindrances and accumulating merit so that a disciple will have success in the practice of tantra.

preta (Skt). Or hungry ghost. One of the six classes of samsaric beings, pretas experience the greatest sufferings of hunger and thirst.

puja (Skt). Literally, "offering"; a religious ceremony.

purification. The removal, or cleansing, of negative karma and its imprints from the mind.

refuge. The heartfelt reliance upon Buddha, Dharma, and Sangha for guidance on the path to enlightenment.

renunciation. The state of mind wishing to be liberated from samsara because of not having for even a second the slightest attraction to samsaric perfections.

resultant path. The tantric path, in which the resultant state of Buddhahood is used as the basis of meditational practice.

Reting Monastery. The first Kadampa monastery, built by Dromtönpa in 1057.

righteous conduct of listening. The respectful manner of listening to Dharma teachings; for example, one does not stretch one's legs towards the teacher or altar.

Rinpoche (Tib). Literally, "precious one." An honorific term usually given to recognized reincarnate lamas; a respectful title used for one's own lama.

rupakaya (Skt). The pure body of an enlightened being, of which there are two aspects: sambhogakaya and nirmanakaya.

samatha (Skt). Or, in Tibetan, shi-ne; calm abiding; a state of concentration in which the mind is able to abide steadily, without effort and for as long as desired, on an object of meditation.

samsara (Skt). Cyclic existence; the six realms: the lower realms of the hell beings, hungry ghosts, and animals, and the upper realms of the humans, demi-gods, and gods; the recurring cycle of death and rebirth within one or other of the six realms under the control of karma and delusions; also refers to the contaminated aggregates of a sentient being.

Sangha (Skt). The third object of refuge; absolute Sangha are those who have directly realized emptiness; relative Sangha are ordained monks and nuns.

sentient being. Any being who has not yet reached enlightenment.

Sera Monastery. One of the three great Gelug monasteries and situated 5 km north of Lhasa, Sera was founded in 1419 by Jamchen Chöje, a disciple of Lama Tsong Khapa. A Sera in exile has been established in South India.

Shantideva (685–763). The great Indian scholar and bodhisattva who wrote *A Guide to the Bodhisattva's Way of Life,* one of the essential Mahayana texts.

six realms. The realms of gods, demi-gods, humans, animals, pretas, and hell beings.

stupa (Skt). A reliquary representing the Buddha's mind.

suffering of change. What is normally regarded as pleasure, which because of its transitory nature sooner or later turns into suffering.

suffering of suffering. The commonly recognized suffering experiences of pain, discomfort, and unhappiness.

suffering migratory being. A being born in the animal, preta, or hell realms.

sutra (Skt). The Hinayana and Paramitayana discourses of the Buddha; a scriptural text and the teachings and practices it contains.

tantra (Skt). The esoteric discourses of Buddha; a scriptural text and the teachings and practices it contains. Tantric practices generally involve identification of oneself with a fully enlightened deity in order to transform one's impure states of body, speech, and mind into the pure state of an enlightened being.

Tantrayana (Skt). See *Vajrayana.*

Tara (Skt). A female meditational deity that embodies the enlightened activity of the Buddhas; often referred to as the mother of the Buddhas of the past, present, and future.

ten richnesses. The ten qualities that characterize a perfect human rebirth: (1) being born as a human being; (2) being born in a Dharma country; (3) being born with perfect mental and physical faculties; (4) being free of the five uninterrupted negative karmas; (5) having faith in the Buddha's teachings;

(6) being born when a Buddha has descended; (7) being born when the teachings have been revealed; (8) being born when the teachings are still alive; (9) being born when there are still followers of the teachings; (10) having the necessary conditions to practice Dharma.

Tengyur (Tib). The part of the Tibetan Buddhist canon that contains commentaries by Indian pandits on the discourses of Buddha.

thought training. See *thought transformation*.

thought transformation. Or, in Tibetan, lo-jong. A powerful approach to the development of bodhicitta, in which the mind is trained to use all situations, both happy and unhappy, as a means to destroy self-cherishing.

three poisonous minds. Ignorance, anger, and attachment.

three principal aspects of the path. The essential teachings of the lam-rim: renunciation, bodhicitta, and emptiness.

three realms. The desire, form, and formless realms.

three visions. Subtle states of mind experienced, for example, at the time of death, and utilized in meditation by accomplished tantric practitioners.

true existence. The type of existence that everything appears to possess; in fact, everything is empty of true existence. (See *emptiness*.)

Tsong Khapa, Lama (1357–1419). The revered teacher and accomplished practitioner who founded the Gelug order of Tibetan Buddhism. An emanation of Manjushri, the Buddha of Wisdom.

unification of no more learning. The ultimate achievement, Buddhahood.

upper realms. The god, demi-god, and human realms.

Vajrasattva (Skt). A tantric deity used in purification practices.

Vajrayana (Skt). Also known as Tantrayana, or Mantrayana. The quickest vehicle of Buddhism, capable of leading to the attainment of full enlightenment within one lifetime.

Wheel-turning King. Or Universal Monarch; a powerful king who propagates the Dharma.

Yamantaka (Skt). The wrathful male deity who is the tantric manifestation of Manjushri, Buddha of Wisdom.

yogi (Skt). A highly realized meditator.

Bibliography of Works Cited

1. Sūtras and Tantras

Heart of Wisdom Sutra (The Essence of Wisdom)
Prajñāhṛdaya/Bhagavatīprajñāpāramitāhṛdayasūtra
Shes rab snying po/bCom ldan 'das ma shes rab kyi pha rol
tu phyin pa'i snying po'i mdo
Translated by Donald S. Lopez, Jr., *The Heart Sūtra
Explained* (Albany: SUNY, 1988)

2. Sanskrit and Tibetan Treatises

Atīsha (982–1054)
Lamp on the Path to Enlightenment
Bodhipathapradīpa
Byang chub lam gyi sgron ma
Translated by Richard Sherburne in *A Lamp for the Path
and Commentary* (London: Allen and Unwin, 1983)

Chandrakīrti (Zla-ba-grags-pa)
Supplement to (Nāgārjuna's) "Treatise on the Middle Way"
Madhyamakāvatāra
dbU ma la 'jug pa
Translated by C. W. Huntington, Jr. with Geshe Namgyal
Wangchen in *The Emptiness of Emptiness* (Honolulu:
University of Hawaii Press, 1989)

Lodrö Gyaltsen (1402–1471)
Opening the Door of Dharma: The Initial Stage of Training the Mind in the Graduated Path to Enlightenment
   Byang chub lam gyi rim pa la blo sbyong ba la thok mar blo sbyong ba chos kyi sgo 'byed

Maitreya (Byams-pa)
Ornament for Clear Realization
   Abhisamayālaṃkāra
   mNgon par rtogs pa'i rgyan
   Translated by E. Conze, *Abhisamayālaṅkāra*, Serie
      Orientale Roma VI (Rome: IS.M.E.O., July 1954)

Nāgārjuna (kLu-sgrub)
Letter to a Friend
   Suhṛllekha
   bShes pa'i spring yig
   Translation by Geshe L. Tharchin and A.B.Engle,
      Nāgārjuna's Letter (Dharamsala: LTWA, 1979)

The Precious Garland of Advice for the King
   Rājāparikathāratnāvalī
   rGyal po la gtam bya ba rin po che'i phreng ba
   Translated by Jeffrey Hopkins in *The Buddhism of Tibet*
      (Ithaca: Snow Lion, 1987)

Pabongka Rinpoche (1871–1941)
Liberation in the Palm of Your Hand
   rNam sgrol lag bcangs su gtod pa'i man ngag zab mo tshang la ma nor ba mtshungs med chos kyi rgyal po'i thugs bcud byang chub lam gyi rim pa'i nyams khrid kyi zin bris gsung rab kun gyi bcud bsdus gdams ngag bdud rtsi'i snying po
   Translated by Michael Richards, *Liberation in the Palm of Your Hand* (Boston: Wisdom, 1991)

Panchen Lama Losang Chökyi Gyaltsen (1569–1662)
Guru Puja, The
Zab lam bla ma mchod pa'i cho ga bde stong dbyer med
me dang tshogs mchod bcad
Translated and published by the Library of Tibetan Works
and Archives (Dharamsala: LTWA, 1979)

Commentary on the Lam drön (*Lamp on the Path to Enlightenment* by Atīsha)
Byang chub lam gyi sgron ma'i rnam bshad phul byung
bzhal pa'i dga' ston
Translated by Richard Sherburne (*see* Atīsha, *above*).

Purbu jok Jampa Gyatso (1825–1901)
*Collected Topics/Presentation of Collected Topics Revealing the
Meaning of the Texts on Valid Cognition, the Magical Key to the
Path of Reasoning*
Tshad ma'i gzhung don 'byed pa'i bsdus grva'i rnam bzhag
rigs lam 'phrul gyi lde mig
Partially translated by Daniel E. Perdue in *Debate in
Tibetan Buddhism* (Ithaca: Snow Lion, 1992)

Shāntideva (Zhi ba lha) (685–763)
A Guide to the Bodhisattva's Way of Life
Bodhisattvacaryāvatāra
Byang chub sems dpa'i spyod pa la 'jug pa
Translated by Stephen Batchelor, *A Guide to the Bodhi-
sattva's Way of Life* (Dharamsala: LTWA, 1979)

Tsong Khapa (1357–1419)
The Foundation of All Good Qualities
Yon tan bzhi gyur ma
Translated by Glenn H. Mullin in "A *Lam-rim* Preliminary
Rite," in the Third Dalai Lama and Glenn H. Mullin,

Essence of Refined Gold (Ithaca: Snow Lion, 1982)

Great Exposition of the Stages of the Path (The Great Commentary on the Graduated Path to Enlightenment)
Lam rim chen mo/sKyes bu gsum gyi rnyams su blang ba'i rim pa thams cad tshang bar ston pa'i byang chub lam gyi rim pa
Partial translation by A. Wayman, *Calming the Mind and Discerning the Real* (New York: Columbia, 1978)

Suggested Further Reading

Batchelor, Stephen, ed. *The Jewel in the Lotus.* Boston: Wisdom Publications, 1987.

Chang, Garma C. C., trans. *The Hundred Thousand Songs of Milarepa.* Vols. 1 and 2. Boston: Shambhala Publications, 1979.

Chödrön, Pema. *The Wisdom of No Escape and the Path of Loving-Kindness.* Boston: Shambhala Publications, 1991.

Chodron, Thubten. *Open Heart, Clear Mind.* Ithaca: Snow Lion Publications, 1991.

Dhargyey, Geshe Ngawang. *An Anthology of Well-Spoken Advice.* Translated by Sharpa Tulku. Edited by Alexander Berzin. Dharamsala: Library of Tibetan Works and Archives, 1982.

_____. *Tibetan Tradition of Mental Development.* Dharamsala: Library of Tibetan Works and Archives, 1985.

Dharmarakshita. *The Wheel of Sharp Weapons.* Translation and commentary by Geshe Dhargyey, et al. Dharamsala: Library of Tibetan Works and Archives, 1976.

Gyatso, Tenzin, the Fourteenth Dalai Lama. *Freedom in Exile.* New York: HarperCollins, 1990.

_____. *Kindness, Clarity and Insight.* Ithaca: Snow Lion Publications, 1984.

_____. *The Meaning of Life From a Buddhist Perspective.* Translated and edited by Jeffrey Hopkins. Boston: Wisdom Publications, 1992.

_____. *Opening the Eye of New Awareness.* Translated by

Donald S. Lopez, Jr. Boston: Wisdom Publications, 1985.

_____. *The Buddhism of Tibet.* Translated and edited by Jeffrey Hopkins. Ithaca: Snow Lion Publications, 1987.

Gyatso, Tenzin, the Fourteenth Dalai Lama et al. *MindScience: An East-West Dialogue.* Edited by Daniel Goleman and Robert A. F. Thurman. Boston: Wisdom Publications, 1991.

Hopkins, Jeffrey. *The Tantric Distinction: An Introduction to Tibetan Buddhism.* Edited by Anne C. Klein. Boston: Wisdom Publications, 1984.

Kongtrul, Jamgon. *The Great Path of Awakening.* Boston: Shambhala, 1988.

Levey, Joel and Michelle. *The Fine Arts of Relaxation, Concentration and Meditation.* Boston: Wisdom Publications, 1987.

Lhalungpa, Lobsang, trans. *The Life of Milarepa.* New York: Arkana, 1992.

McDonald, Kathleen. *How to Meditate.* Edited by Robina Courtin. Boston: Wisdom Publications, 1984.

Pabongka Rinpoche. *Liberation in the Palm of Your Hand.* Edited in the Tibetan by Trijang Rinpoche. Translated by Michael Richards. Boston: Wisdom Publications, 1991.

Rabten, Geshe. *The Essential Nectar; Meditations on the Buddhist Path.* Editing and verse translation by Martin Willson. Boston: Wisdom Publications, 1984.

_____. *Treasury of Dharma: A Tibetan Buddhist Meditation Course.* Translated by Gonsar Rinpoche. Edited by Brian Grabia. London: Tharpa Publications, 1988.

_____ and Dhargyey, Geshe Ngawang. *Advice from a Spiritual Friend: Buddhist Thought Transformation.* Translated and edited by Brian Beresford. Boston: Wisdom Publications, 1984.

Shantideva. *A Guide to the Bodhisattva's Way of Life.* Translated by Stephen Batchelor. Dharamsala: Library of Tibetan Works and Archives, 1981.

Thondup Rinpoche, Tulku. *Enlightened Living.* Boston: Shambhala Publications, 1991.

Thurman, Robert, ed. *Life and Teachings of Tsong Khapa.* Dharamsala: Library of Tibetan Works and Archives, 1982.

Trungpa, Chögyam. *Cutting Through Spiritual Materialism.* Edited by John Baker and Marvin Casper. Boston: Shambhala Publications, 1973.

Tsongkapa. *The Principal Teachings of Buddhism.* Translated by Geshe Lobsang Tharchin with Michael Roach. New Jersey, Mahayana Sutra and Tantra Press, 1988.

Wallace, B. Alan. *Tibetan Buddhism From the Ground Up.* Boston: Wisdom Publications, 1993.

Wangchen, Geshe Namgyal. *Awakening the Mind of Enlightenment: Meditations on the Buddhist Path.* Boston: Wisdom Publications, 1987.

Wangyal, Geshe. *The Door of Liberation.* (New edition.) Boston: Wisdom Publications, 1994.

_____. *The Jewelled Staircase.* Ithaca: Snow Lion Publications, 1986.

Yeshe, Lama Thubten. *Introduction to Tantra: A Vision of Totality.* Compiled and edited by Jonathan Landaw. Boston: Wisdom Publications, 1987.

_____ and Zopa Rinpoche. *Wisdom Energy.* Boston: Wisdom Publications, 1987.

Zopa Rinpoche, Lama. *Transforming Problems Into Happiness.* Edited by Ailsa Cameron and Robina Courtin. Boston: Wisdom Publications, 1993.

WISDOM PUBLICATIONS

Wisdom Publications is a non-profit publisher of books on Buddhism, Tibet, and related East-West themes. Our titles are published in appreciation of Buddhism as a living philosophy and with the special commitment to preserve and transmit important works from all the major Buddhist traditions.

If you would like more information or a copy of our mail order catalogue, and to be kept informed about future publications, please write to us at: 361 Newbury Street, Boston, Massachusetts, 02115, USA.

THE WISDOM TRUST

As a non-profit publisher, Wisdom is dedicated to the publication of fine Dharma books for the benefit of all sentient beings. We depend upon sponsors in order to publish books like the one you are holding in your hand.

If you would like to make a donation to the Wisdom Trust Fund to help us continue our Dharma work or to receive information about opportunities for planned giving, please write to our Boston office.

Thank you so much.

Wisdom is a non-profit, charitable 501(c)(3) organization and a part of the Foundation for the Preservation of the Mahayana Tradition (FPMT).

THE FOUNDATION FOR THE PRESERVATION OF THE MAHAYANA TRADITION

The Foundation for the Preservation of the Mahayana Tradition (FPMT) is an international network of Buddhist centers and activities dedicated to the transmission of Mahayana Buddhism as a practiced and living tradition. The FPMT was founded in 1975 by Lama Thubten Yeshe and Lama Thubten Zopa Rinpoche. It is composed of monasteries, retreat centers, communities, city teaching centers, publishing houses, and healing centers, all working to benefit others. Teachings, such as those presented in *The Door to Satisfaction*, are given at many of these centers.

To receive a complete listing of these centers as well as news about the activities throughout this global network, please request a complimentary copy of the MANDALA journal from:

FPMT CENTRAL OFFICE
P. O. Box 1778
Soquel, California 95073
Telephone: (408) 476–8435
Fax: (408) 476–4823

CARE OF DHARMA BOOKS

Dharma books contain the teachings of the Buddha; they have the power to protect against lower rebirth and to point the way to liberation. Therefore, they should be treated with respect—kept off the floor and places where people sit or walk—and not stepped over. They should be covered or protected for transporting and kept in a high, clean place separate from more "mundane" materials. Other objects should not be placed on top of Dharma books and materials. Licking the fingers to turn pages is considered bad form (and negative karma). If it is necessary to dispose of Dharma materials, they should be burned rather than thrown in the trash. When burning Dharma, first recite OM, AH, HUNG. Then, visualize the letters of the texts (to be burned) absorbing into the AH, and that absorbing into you. After that, you can burn the texts.

These considerations may also be kept in mind for Dharma artwork, as well as the written teachings and artwork of other religions.

Also by Lama Zopa Rinpoche

Books

Transforming Problems Into Happiness

Lama Zopa literally teaches us how to be happy when we are not, by bringing about the changes in attitude that permit us to live happy and relaxed lives in which external circumstances no longer rule us.

"This ancient technique [thought transformation] is given a fresh and practical treatment here. This book should be read as the words of a wise, loving parent.... A masterfully brief statement of Buddhist teachings on the nature of humanity and human suffering... Zopa Rinpoche is a wise and inspiring teacher."
  —Utne Reader

"Lama Zopa states that through contemplation on an altruistic attitude, we can take joy in the challenge of being truly kind in an unhappy world."
  —Shambhala Sun

"'This small volume contains a wealth of wisdom."
  —The Beacon

88pp, $10

WISDOM ENERGY: BASIC BUDDHIST TEACHINGS
Lama Thubten Yeshe and Lama Zopa Rinpoche

Written with characteristic warmth and directness, this book is a simple yet compelling introduction to Buddhism going to the heart of Buddhist practice.

"This is a superb book. With great lucidity and clarity these two Tibetan masters present basic Buddhist teachings to a western audience. Highly recommended."
   —Resource

"…immensely practical advice and suggestions. Meditators will find the book very helpful. Highly recommended to all Buddhists."
   —The Middle Way

151pp, $10

Transcripts

THE KINDNESS OF THE GURU

Lama Zopa tells how he first met his teacher, Lama Yeshe, and describes the many exceptional ways in which Lama Yeshe was kind, dedicating his life to the service of others.

61pp, $6

TARA THE LIBERATOR

This small volume explains vividly to practitioners and newcomers alike the qualities and characteristics of Tara, and how one can engage in her practice.

31pp, $4

These and other Dharma books, including those listed in the Suggested Further Reading list, are available from Wisdom Publications.